Praise for *Opening the Gates*

"This bold and impassioned book offers a clear-headed and unfailing perceptive analysis of the relationship between welcoming converts and a healthy Jewish future. The book should be required reading for all concerned about that future."

—Lawrence J. Epstein, president,
Conversion to Judaism Resource Center

"As Tobin promises at the outset of this provocative and stimulating book, his is a controversial thesis. But it comes from one of the most articulate thinkers on the subject, and as such, anyone seriously interested in the future of American Jewish life simply must factor this well-written work into their own thinking."

—Dr. Daniel Gordis, dean, Ziegler School of Rabbinic Studies,
author of *Does the World Need the Jews?:
Rethinking Chosenness and American Jewish Identity*

"Gary Tobin offers a revolutionary challenge to the American Jewish community—to become proactive in seeking converts. What this book offers other religious groups, however, is solid thinking about achieving and maintaining religious identity in the midst of a pluralistic culture, and what 'conversion' means in such a culture. Any leader of an American congregation of any faith will find provocative ideas here."

—The Rev. Loren B. Mead, founding president,
The Alban Institute, Inc.

"Gary Tobin has written the most important and challenging book in American Jewish public policy in years. People may agree or disagree, but no one interested in contemporary Jewish life will be able to ignore this work."

—Steven L. Spiegel, professor of political science, UCLA

"In this volume Gary Tobin, a leading light in Jewish communal research, bravely moves beyond academic description and analysis and embraces a provocative solution for American Jewry's continuity problem—a proactive conversion policy. Tobin firmly advocates that American Jewry cannot allow blind forces to determine its destiny but instead it must create its own future out of the social realities of the present—it is an enticing vision that all concerned Jews should seriously consider."
—Dr. Barry A. Kosmin, director of research,
Institute for Jewish Policy Research

"An important book, both passionate and pragmatic, that does not cry Cassandra but recognizes the positive potentiality for Jewish renewal through programs and designs of proactive conversion. The author is involved in his subject, as both analyst and advocate. This lucidly written book is significant for serious rabbinic and lay Jews and their institutions who recognize the urgent need to redefine and revitalize Judaism and the character of Jewish peoplehood."
—Rabbi Harold M. Schulweis,
Valley Beth Shalom, Encino, California

"Only someone like Dr. Gary Tobin who is so well informed on the demography of American Jewry, could call as desperately and as unequivocally as he does for a program of 'reaching out.' There is a feeling that something can be done besides witnessing the disappearance of American Jewry, and in that sense it is one of the most optimistic books written on the subject."
—Yossi Beilin, Member of the Knesset

"*Opening the Gates* is a truthful and insightful analysis of the current issues facing the American Jewish community. Dr. Gary Tobin presents innovative ideas and new approaches to revitalizing American Judaism in the twenty-first century."
—Rabbi Neal Weinberg, University of Judaism

"Gary Tobin gives us a fresh, top-to-bottom investigation of attitudes and practices regarding conversion of non-Jews. All Jewish leaders will benefit from this analysis of options and consequences."
—Dean Hoge, The Catholic University of America

A gift from

Marty Wolk

TEMPLE BETH AM
Seattle

Opening the Gates

Opening the Gates

How Proactive Conversion Can Revitalize the Jewish Community

Gary A. Tobin

Jossey-Bass Publishers
San Francisco

Excerpt from *Conversion to Judaism* by Lawrence J. Epstein reprinted by permission of the publisher, Jason Aronson Inc., Northvale, NJ © 1996.

Jossey-Bass books and products are available through most bookstores. To contact Jossey-Bass directly, call (888) 378-2537, fax to (800) 605-2665, or visit our website at www.josseybass.com.

Substantial discounts on bulk quantities of Jossey-Bass books are available to corporations, professional associations, and other organizations. For details and discount information, contact the special sales department at Jossey-Bass.

 Manufactured in the United States of America on Lyons Falls Turin Book. This paper is acid-free and 100 percent totally chlorine-free.

Library of Congress Cataloging-in-Publication Data

Tobin, Gary A.
  Opening the gates : how proactive conversion can revitalize the Jewish community / Gary A. Tobin. — 1st ed.
      p.   cm.
    Includes bibliographical references and index.
    ISBN 0-7879-0881-9 (acid-free paper)
  1. Proselytes and proselyting, Jewish. 2. Judaism—United States.
I. Title.
BM729.P7 T63   1999
296.6'9—dc21   98-51233

FIRST EDITION
HB Printing   10 9 8 7 6 5 4 3 2 1

Contents

—To Diane Kaufmann Tobin, born into a family with two generations of mixed marriage and raised an Episcopalian, who chose to nurture her own Jewish identity over a period of many years before her ritual conversion to Judaism at the mikvah at age thirty

—To Sarah Kaufmann Weinberg and Aryeh Kaufmann Weinberg, who took a swim in the mikvah at ages six and three

—To Mia Kaufmann Weinberg, born of two Jewish parents, who took the trip to the mikvah while still in the womb

—To Adam Zev Tobin and Amy Rebecca Tobin, born of two born-Jewish parents

—To Jonah Kaufmann Tobin, eighteen months old, born of non-Jewish birthparents, adopted at one day old, who had a bris at eight days and a double dunk in the mikvah at eight months

Preface

Few subjects in Jewish life are as controversial as conversion to Judaism. Intermarriage, assimilation, antisemitism, religious pluralism, and control of religious authority in Israel all come into play. No subject could provoke as much debate about more matters of profound importance and meaning to Jews.

Hundreds of books have been written over the last few years about all of these subjects. Yet books specifically about conversion are glaringly absent. An occasional debate in a Jewish magazine or an opinion piece in a newspaper appears, but the millions of words about intermarriage, assimilation, pluralism, and the future of the Jewish community do not include much about conversion—especially proactive conversion among non-Jews to become Jews. *Opening the Gates* focuses specifically on conversion.

I might be taken to task by some people because I am not a rabbi or because this book does not engage in an interpretive discussion of what the Torah, Talmud, and later commentaries say about intermarriage and conversion. Those modes of inquiry and analysis, debated by individuals far more qualified and knowledgeable than I am, constitute a literature of their own. I write from the perspective of a social scientist, not that of a religious scholar or leader.

It is important to say what this book does not purport to do. Although brief allusions are made to historical events and processes, this is not a history of conversion in ancient, medieval, or modern times, either *to* Judaism or *from* Judaism. Nor is it about the theology of conversion, the rabbinic interpretations of why Jews must refuse or accept converts. Rather, this book examines the role that conversion should play in the Jewish future. It looks at how the Jewish community currently handles issues of intermarriage and conversion and recommends strategies to incorporate conversion into a larger vision of building the next Jewish civilization.

The objections to proactive conversion fall into basically three categories. This first is emotional—fear and anxiety about the repercussions from the non-Jewish world. We are afraid of what might happen, what kind of reaction we might unleash. The emotional response is a conditioned one; conversion, violence, and terror are closely linked in the Jewish psyche. The second category of objections is strategic and tactical, including arguments that we should spend money, time, and effort on the more affiliated and identified Jews before we try to bring in anybody else. The third set of objections is religious: arguments that Jewish law or tradition limits or prohibits proactive conversion, depending on various interpretations.

All of these objections weave into one another and together pose a formidable set of barriers to thinking about proactive conversion. We have to confront all of these concerns if proactive conversion is to become a reality in Jewish life.

The research for this book was extensive, spanning many years. Hundreds of documents in the Reform, Conservative, and other movements were assembled and analyzed. Hundreds of interviews were conducted with rabbis, institutional representatives, and ordinary citizens trying to sort out their Jewish lives. Surveys were conducted with congregations. I listened carefully to the voices of people in the Jewish community who make policy guidelines and decisions and those who are affected by these collective thoughts and actions.*

---

*All uncredited quotations, anecdotes, and vignettes that appear in this book are based on personal interviews or personal correspondence via mail or e-mail. The names and identifying characteristics of the persons described have been changed wherever prudent. I thank all these individuals for having granted me permission to use their words.

I have grown weary of the obsessive focus on intermarriage. Too much talk about intermarriage creates background noise. The banging and clanging about the topic and the energy it absorbs confuse strategic thinking about how to be a better Jewish community. Can Jews forge a joyful, nurturing, meaningful, and exciting religious and cultural existence while focusing on doom?

My criticism of the prevention strategy—avoiding the question of conversion entirely by preventing intermarriage—is grounded in part in my conclusion that such an approach has already failed and will fail in the future. Furthermore, I do not believe that all mixed marriages will result in a conversion, no matter how proactive we are or what strategies we employ. Some individuals believe in Christ or Buddha, some do not believe in religion at all, and some do not want to hurt members of their families by rejecting their religion. We can do much better among those who could be candidates for Judaism. I believe there are better ways to think about intermarriage than prevention. However, I never suggest that the growing number of mixed marriages is inconsequential. I say throughout the book that I do not believe that mixed marriages strengthen Jewish life— quite the opposite. This book, after all, is a case for conversion, the creation of unambiguous Jewish households.

We need to talk about conversion, its limits and possibilities. The community needs to focus on new and different ways to grow. I am not a participant in the optimism-versus-pessimism debates about Judaism's future. Both stances require being something of an ideologue.

I am neither optimistic nor pessimistic, nor am I an ideologue. The Jewish community shows signs of vibrancy, and it shows signs of stagnation. It reveals openness to new ideas and experimentation, while it also reveals rigidity and resistance to innovation. Some aspects of the Jewish communal structure show creativity, and some show burdensome bureaucratic gridlock in developing new approaches and programs to serve the Jewish community.

Too much optimism and too much pessimism both seem to lead to the same dead end. On the one hand, being overly optimistic engenders complacency and self-congratulation. "We are doing just fine, thank you. Look how wonderful everything is and will be." The sunny outlook keeps us from asking hard questions and dealing with the truly complex and puzzling issues that arise from rapid and accumulated change: we do not act effectively because we do not feel the need.

The pessimists, the doom-and-gloom crowd, are just as likely to create paralysis. "If defeat and destruction are around the corner, why bother?" While the optimists tend to want to leave well enough alone, the pessimists want to go backward, because it seems safer to rely on what is known.

Although neither optimist nor pessimist, I am a pragmatist. I believe change is necessary and possible to achieve; but it comes hard, meets all kinds of resistance, takes a long time to happen, and often is not everything we plan or hope to achieve. But some progress is better than none, and moving forward is success, even if a whole vision does not take form at once.

The Jewish community must redefine itself, investing in the actual vision, design, and implementation functions needed to remake itself. What the community desperately needs is a new institutional framework in which visionary leaders can work to help direct and mold the future of Jewish life. Some of this investment is already taking place in grassroots organizations and institutions, programs, and projects springing up all over the United States. Programs within existing institutions and outside them show incredible promise for redefining the Jewish future. We need to increase such efforts. Breaking the constraints of the current system—investing in the new, the odd, the different, and the strange—remolds the Jewish community.

Most of the arguments that oppose creativity are rooted in the belief that the Jewish community has limited financial resources to expend. Therefore, it is argued that everyone must be very circumspect on how scarce resources are institutionally and programmatically allocated. This tautology, however, is one of the most restrictive in contemporary Jewish life. Plenty of money is available. Indeed, Jews give away billions of dollars for philanthropic purposes every year, to both Jewish and non-Jewish institutions. Furthermore, the Jewish community is sitting on tens of billions of dollars in foundation assets. We have vast resources that could be expended for Jewish community building.

Thus it is not the lack of financial resources that plagues the Jewish community but the lack of ideas, of venues in which to implement those ideas, and of visionary individuals and a core body of professionals to make change happen. Most observers in the Jewish community believe that a lack of money inhibits change when the opposite is true! A lack of change inhibits the mustering of financial resources. If the right ideas, programs, and institutions are invented and promoted, the dollars will be found to support them. Continuing to rely on the same programs over and over again hobbles inspiration. Continuing to emphasize ideologies and strategies that have failed in the past creates cynicism and reluctance to take bold initiatives.

I believe we need more Jews, and more connected Jews. I believe that the time is right to make the community grow through proactive conversion. I know the subject is fraught with controversy; all visions of alternative futures are beset by doubts, and the opponents of "strange" ideas raise loud protests. If these ideas about proactive conversion are bad or untenable, so be it. But we need to think about it, talk about it, and wrestle with it, even if we decide not to take action.

This book makes some harsh assessments. I do not think much of most of the current Jewish education system. There are gems here and there, among institutions, programs, and teachers. But we need a major retooling. We have known this for many years and have not yet made the intellectual or financial investment to change what we know has to be done. We know that many of our synagogue worship services need an overhaul. We know that much of the community-building, identity-formation agenda requires more attention.

We know that we do not do much for eighteen-to-thirty-year-old Jews, who are largely detached from Jewish life. These are just some of the major issues.

I can hear the critics already. "Author slams Jewish education." "Author criticizes synagogues." "Author is unfair to rabbis." "Author says intermarriage is not a threat to the Jews." They will raise a hue and cry so as not to hear that we must devise systems that acknowledge successful integration, account for it, plan for it, and use it to build a stronger Jewish community. We cannot go on pretending that the organized Jewish community does not need fundamental change.

I have become impatient. Mostly, we fiddle at the margins. We need a communal revolt, and yet we plod along. That is how I *feel*.

What I *think* is that we are making slow and steady progress, and the signs of change are everywhere. New institutions are cropping up; innovative programs are blooming throughout the country. I see the move forward. I want it to be faster and more comprehensive.

I do not believe we can stem the tide of assimilation. I even disdain the language that is used to insist on it. What I want is to understand what it means to be integrated and make the best of it. It is possible for Jews to integrate and yet remain unique. Allusions to Jews disappearing as they did in past societies are meaningless; no place has been like America in terms of religious pluralism, technological influence, and a host of other factors. We can draw on history for understanding, but we are foolish to be constrained and daunted by it.

This book is meant to stir things up. I want it to spark a vociferous debate that leads the Jewish community to focus on and invest in conversion. I want to encourage an institutional commitment to creating more Jews. I want to ask hard questions, new questions, and even some questions that others may call silly. I would rather risk putting forth some crazy ideas than be crippled by cries of "It won't work," "It costs too much," "We never did this before," "We don't have the money," "We should try something else first," and "What if it fails?" Over time, many crazy ideas are vindicated; some turn out to be just crazy. Which is which cannot be determined without considering them all.

This book is likely to cause discomfort, perhaps disdain, maybe even some anger. I am deeply committed to improving the quality of Jewish life—as indeed are those who will disagree with me. That common bond should not be forgotten.

That is what I truly love about Judaism and being Jewish. Monotheism was a crazy idea. Social justice was a crazy idea. Universal literacy was a crazy idea. Israel was a crazy idea. Being on the edge—pushing the new and profound—leads to advances in theology, social structure, medicine, the arts, and all realms of human existence. How invigorating and meaningful life is for the craziness of being a Jew and the role Judaism plays in the world.

Who I am is defined by Judaism. It is my work, my life. I love being a Jew. I understand what a historical triumph it is for me to feel that way and say it in these words so that any other Jew or Gentile can read them. My children love being Jews. They are proud to be who they are. I feel secure in America. I feel secure because Israel exists, in spite of its problems.

I wrote this book because I see people all around me who would be Jews—if we helped them. I see spouses of Jews who are intrigued and looking for religious security. They could be Jews. I see my children's friends, who have no religion of their own and come to our Passover Seder every year. They eat and breathe Judaism in so many ways. They could be Jews. I meet people on airplanes or at conferences who (I learn after a few minutes of conversation in which they find out what I do) have a Jewish father or Jewish grandmother and are fascinated by Judaism. They could be Jews. I see millions of Jewish lives unrealized. This seems to me an individual and communal shame. I wrote this book so we can think about how to provide a gateway for all of these millions who would be Jews.

The issue is not whether Jews and Judaism survive but whether it matters. Judaism as a religion and the Jews as a people have been enormously influential at different times throughout history. As the world shrinks through technology, and population grows and other groups prosper, the influence of the Jews is in question. What do we have to offer? Will we be distinctive, interesting, and powerful enough to make a difference?

Acknowledgments

This book could not have been finished without the work of Scott Rubin, who was instrumental in helping me complete the chapters on structural barriers and models of success and edit the book. Laureen Kim prepared the manuscript, not only with a technical eye but also with keen insight into the substance of the book. Kathy Candito managed to keep life in order while the book was being finished. Steven Spiegel read the manuscript more than once, and his comments were extremely useful. Sarah Polster at Jossey-Bass was a wonderful source of ideas that shaped the book. Diane Kaufmann Tobin's emotional vision and probing intellect helped guide my thinking about this book. Her love for Judaism, her choice to reclaim the identity her family abandoned, her journey in becoming a Jew—these things inspire me. Her story reaffirms that Jewish life is filled with joyful, purposeful, passionate possibilities.

San Francisco   Gary A. Tobin
January, 1999

Opening the Gates

1

A Community in Transition

The Jewish community is hysterical about Jews marrying non-Jews. The language of tragedy and despair pervades analysis and discussion of what is called the "intermarriage crisis" in America today. Denominations within Judaism have passed bellicose resolutions calling for prevention of intermarriage; and respected scholars, rabbinic leaders, and popular culture figures in Jewish life consistently liken intermarriage to disease, war, and genocide (self-inflicted or otherwise). In an article examining intermarriage in America, Rabbi Ephraim Buchwald, founder of the National Jewish Outreach Program, warns, "There are no barking dogs and no Zyklon-B gas . . . but make no mistake: this is a spiritual Holocaust" (Horowitz, 1997, p. 36).

With the exception of Israel, no other issue captures as much attention, discussion, and debate in Jewish life. Millions of words and kilowatts of human energy—lectures and sermons at synagogues, books and articles, op-ed pieces, and how-to manuals—focus on the causes and consequences of this looming threat to our future. Even as we debate its origins, Jewish organizations and institutions are scrambling to devise and implement programs to solve the intermarriage crisis before it is too late. But they are doomed to fail, because *there is no intermarriage crisis in the United States today.*

Tribal Threat and Personal Loss

Certainly, the issue of Jews marrying Gentiles is demographically real. The rate of Jewish marriages to non-Jews has risen from practically zero in the early 1950s to about 50 percent in 1990 (Council of Jewish Federations, 1992). Some scholars debate whether the rate is 42 percent or 52 percent, but no matter. The incidence is vastly higher than it was a generation ago, particularly for Reform Jews, Jews in the western United States, and children of mixed marriages. We do not know if rates of intermarriage are still increasing, but it is clear that intermarriage has become commonplace in American Jewish life.

Because intermarriage has grown to such proportions, we fear that the Jewish community is free-falling into tribal disintegration. The idea of Jews marrying non-Jews engenders a tripartite sense of loss: tribal, institutional, and personal. These losses are real and painful, and we must pay attention to them.

Tribal Loss

As more Jews choose to marry non-Jews, we feel a loss of community, of membership in the tribe. Consistent contact with similar people helps create feelings of familiarity, belonging, and acceptance. We acquire knowledge of place, of what is expected and how to behave through shared experiences. Community grows from having common bonds, mutual responsibility, a sense both of shared destiny and of obligation to take care of one another in fundamental, life-supporting ways. Assimilation into the American culture also creates a sense of comfort but also confusion, because in so doing we embrace strangers who may look, think, or act differently. Many Jews may not know much about Judaism, but we do know that we are somehow different because we are Jews—whatever that means. And we know that other Jews are somehow connected to us.

When an individual marries someone who was not born Jewish, we often feel that the person who intermarries is lost to the community, or that the children or grandchildren might be lost. We experience sadness and a sense of failure: the tribe has a defector, a wanderer, someone who is confused or maybe treacherous, ignorant of the consequences of such a decision or uncaring about the Jewish people. Those who intermarry go to the other side—the *outside*—choosing another people and not our own. When we see too many people leaving the fold, our sense of communal loss becomes severe and traumatic. We see each defection as contributing to the cumulative demise of the group. The sense of tribal loss overwhelms us, and we are saddened that we might be the last members of a dying people, anthropological islanders whose extinction is only a matter of time. It is no surprise, then, that Jewish community leaders often speak of intermarriage in terms of death, warfare, and genocide—concerns of any group, to be sure.

Institutional Loss

A sense of institutional loss also pervades our feelings. Sometimes Jews with non-Jewish spouses choose to bring these strangers into the synagogues, Jewish community centers, and other places where we have traditionally felt safe from outsiders. Some Jews may feel that at least a synagogue should be a secure and secluded place, without having to worry about what one says or does to offend non-Jews. When we feel a sense of institutional loss, we are lamenting that Jewish space is no longer exclusively Jewish. If anyone can come here and participate, we lose our haven.

The sense of institutional loss, however, cuts both ways. Although some people feel threatened because non-Jews participate in Jewish institutions, others feel threatened because the institutions do not attract enough people—those who are married to non-Jews do not come at all. The very survival of the institution is threatened: Who will pay for the infrastructure? Who will fill the halls for events? Who will serve on the boards and committees? Institutions thrive through the financial support of interested members and through the efforts of hundreds of thousands of volunteer

hands. Jews who drift away threaten the lifeblood of the institutional structure. Of course, one does not have to marry a non-Jew
to create this scenario, but mixed-married families tend to be more
institutionally detached than families formed when two Jews marry.
Institutions that feel as if they are fighting to survive place some of
the blame on the intermarriage crisis.

Individual Loss

Individual members of the tribe also experience loss. The problems
of size and meaningfulness of the Jewish community require collective thought and action, but personal losses are not usually addressed
at the communal level. The Jewish community may provide counseling and support services, but the very real pain of individual and
family loss is rarely mitigated through communal response.

The emotional response, the personal one, engulfs our thinking
about the communal response. The sorrow of personal loss overwhelms innovative thinking on how best to address the issue of Jews
marrying non-Jews. Intermarriage becomes the symbol of everything
that is wrong in Jewish life. We raise our voices in anguish, not
because we feel the abstract pain of a community in jeopardy but
rather because we feel the concrete pain of our own threatened family, our own descendants' Jewish oblivion.

Some individuals feel remorseful and guilty that their lives have
not been "Jewish enough" to teach their own children adequately.
They blame themselves for their children's detachment from Jewish
life, especially those whose children have married non-Jews and are
raising non-Jewish children. Some Jews want to create a communal
agenda that builds into others' lives the identity that is lacking in
their own families. They want to prevent for the Jewish community
as a whole what they failed to prevent in their own homes.

Others want to preempt the loss in their own lives. If their children or grandchildren have not yet intermarried, they want to keep
it that way. Some Jews believe that if they build all the bulwarks,

they stave off the personal loss of their own children or grandchildren marrying non-Jews. The hope is a fervent one. The disaster they see engulfing other Jews can be avoided if they build strong enough walls within their families—solid and impervious, to keep away the non-Jewish spouse.

Intermarriage as a Distraction

Emotions around these issues run wild. For some, the sense of foreboding and panic at the prospect of intermarriage, and for others the sense of guilt afterward, guides many individuals into formulating frantic communal strategies of prevention. The fever pitch is frightening, because so many of us Jews are afraid for ourselves, our children, our grandchildren, our siblings, our nephews, and our best friend's children. It is all too close to home.

Ultimately, it is simpler for most Jewish analysts to focus on intermarriage as a communal problem, because it is easier to try to fix the system and talk about communal survival than it is to face loss inside one's own family. The shrillness of the communal war cries about intermarriage encompasses all the sobs of anger, frustration, shame, confusion, disappointment, and resignation about one's own personal life. Jews who feel that they won the intermarriage battle within their own family, who have children and grandchildren married to other Jews, sometimes have a sense of certainty and righteousness: they may stand and offer an enthusiastic "I told you so" with stock answers about what they did right and what others should do.

All of this is not to say that we should not be concerned about intermarriage. We should. We should be concerned about loss of Jewish identity and communal dissolution. Jewish communities throughout the Diaspora are shrinking to one degree or another. Jews who are two or three generations forward from a mixed-married family of a Jew and a non-Jew often carry no recognizable Jewish identity and behavior. The anxiety about Jews marrying non-Jews cannot be dismissed with either "there is no problem," or "everything will be all right," regardless of what we do or do not do. The Jewish community *can* shrink to a marginalized irrelevance.

Jews in Pluralistic America

If we are to devise real solutions to real problems, however, we must examine our concerns in the right context. Intermarriage itself is not the problem. Indeed, we need only look at the hysteria about intermarriage to recognize the depth of our real problem: *we have not yet formulated a set of beliefs, behaviors, and institutional structures that define what it means to be a Jew in the pluralistic society that we ourselves have helped to build.* The integration we sought to achieve and have been so diligent in pursuing seems like a curse to the beneficiaries of freedom and success. The fear of extinction could be a self-fulfilling prophecy for non-Orthodox Judaism. Our worry about the future keeps us from enjoying the successes of the present and feeling secure enough to design the next phase of Jewish civilization.

We are lost and confused. We do not know what to do next. We do not distinguish between *assimilation* and *integration*. (Assimilation is abandonment of traditional religious beliefs and ritual practice. Integration, on the other hand, is maintenance of a separate and distinct set of beliefs and behaviors, *and* adoption of some beliefs and behaviors of the host culture.) It is simpler for us to focus on intermarriage as a symbol of "too much" assimilation, rather than to expend the intellectual, emotional, and financial resources necessary to redefine Jewish life.

This negative focus creates a communal paradox. How can we forge a meaningful religious and cultural existence for ourselves while we focus on the overwhelming pathologies of intermarriage and the decline and destruction caused by too much interaction with other Americans? It is more familiar for many Jews to feel threatened than to think and behave securely, or to build a community based on that security. For some, looking backward feels safer. Some Jews create a nostalgic memory of Jews all marrying each

other, being Torah scholars, and eating bubbie's home-baked chal-
lah. If we can only recapture our unity, our uniqueness, our oneness.
Better to think small. For some, even a degree of antisemitism is
more familiar and more stable than thinking about what Judaism
could and should be. We have a monumental set of tasks before us,
daunting in their complexity and magnitude. It seems simpler and
more manageable to reduce the challenge to one of preventing
intermarriage.

Real Problems

Survival is not growth. Holding our own is not enough. Keeping
destruction at bay is not enough. We must evolve in form and
increase in number and variety, because, as we stand now, the Jewish community is shrinking, both in quantity and in quality. The
quantity is a shrinking population; the quality is a loss of meaningful Jewish identity and communal participation for many Jews. Preventing intermarriage does not resolve these problems, nor does it
help us grow.

The shrinking population is due largely to a static birth rate: too
few Jewish families with too few children. The Jewish community
has not really grown for decades. If not for the continued immigration of Jews from the former Soviet Union, Israel, and elsewhere,
the American Jewish community certainly would be considerably
smaller than it was fifty years ago. Focusing on intermarriage shields
us from having to deal with this issue. The Jewish population would
grow steadily if Jewish families had more children. Well, what if the
community encouraged Jewish families to adopt more children?
There might be other such creative ways to begin thinking about
reversing a shrinking population. We would rather dwell on the loss
from intermarriage, however, than begin the hard job of thinking
about more children.

Loss of meaningful identity is equally hard to address. For many
Jews today, Judaism is simply irrelevant on a daily or weekly basis.
Most of us think of ourselves as Jews, but we are not sure exactly

what that means, or why it is important to us. At the same time, the vast majority of us do not want to stop being Jews. We do not want to call ourselves something else, practice another religion, or remove ourselves entirely from the group. We want to be part of Jewish life, but we are not compelled to do very much about that desire. We may respond to a crisis in Israel or feel empathy if Jews are persecuted in Russia. We provide financial resources to help emigration to Israel and the United States. We attend synagogue on occasion for a few hours and, all things being equal, want a rabbi to marry us, even if our partner is not Jewish.

If the connections to Judaism are tenuous for those who are born Jewish, they often become even more stretched in those families where someone takes a partner who is not born Jewish and who does not convert to Judaism. Of course, the Jewish community does not do much to alter that reality. For many Jews in America, no matter whom we are married to, the connection to Jewish life is shaky.

The real threat when an intermarriage occurs, then, is *not* the non-Jew: *the real threat to our future is the Jew who perceives little meaning in Judaism and who chooses to carry little that is Jewish into the union.* If every Jew married another Jew, the same issues of meaning and commitment would continue to persist. Would the Jewish community be satisfied if all Jews married other Jews, yet the synagogues remained empty (except a couple of times a year), ritual practices were abandoned, and Jews failed to fulfill their mission to perform *mitzvot*? Would it be better if the Jewish community consisted of five-and-a-half million Jews married only to Jews but distanced from meaningful Judaism and withdrawn into a meaningless cult of endogamous monotony? What Judaism *means*—how it is lived, how it influences the lives of Jews and Gentiles alike—is what should matter, not how many Jews marry non-Jews.

Imagining how to infuse Judaism and the Jewish community with meaning is our primary task. We have to confront the mediocrity of many of our Jewish educational experiences. We have to think about how to rebuild Jewish neighborhoods and social groups. We have to think about how boring many synagogue services are and how they drive people away from more participation in Jewish life. There is so much to fix that has little to do with the rate of intermarriage. Nothing is wrong with Judaism; however, we can improve how we deliver it though our institutional world. Yet time and again we make the choice to blame our community problems on the *goyim*—accusing them of stealing our families by marrying us.

Searching Our Souls

We must begin to approach these problems with some healthy soul-searching about the nature and meaning of Jewish identity: who I am and who I am not. How we frame the questions and the answers we come up with constitutes the difference between stagnation and growth. To be sure, our responses need not be a monolithic consensus from the Jewish community. They can be multidimensional in their context, yet consistent in their tone—courageous, proud, and passionate.

We must ask ourselves one central question: How does the Jewish community perpetuate a strong, positive, and meaningful Jewish identity within a pluralistic society? This identity is not only what I *think* and *feel*, but also how I *behave* in relationship to other Jews, to non-Jews, to all living things, to God. How do I define myself distinctively, in a way that is nurturing, protecting, fulfilling, and productive? Judaism has so much to offer in these realms. The communal infrastructure has to be rebuilt to facilitate rather than hinder the expression of a rich Judaism.

We must first examine what we think, in our heart of hearts, about being Jewish. Our language is revealing. To others and among ourselves, we discuss the difficulty of maintaining the religion. We whine about the rigors of *kashrut*, regular synagogue attendance, daily prayer, and other obligations. We sometimes describe Judaism as hard and, by insinuation, burdensome. We are capable of turning relatively joyous occasions such as Passover, a celebration of freedom, into a kvetch about too much matzo. Conversely, how often do we tout the joy and beauty of Judaism, the mystic meanings of the liturgy in Shabbat services, or the sustenance provided by familial and communal support systems? We have internalized a kind of ritual complaining about our own religious practices and beliefs to the point where someone listening to us might wonder why anybody would want to be Jewish.

Self-effacement and self-slander about Jews and Judaism betray our profound lack of self-assurance. Some humor, for example, crosses the line from modesty and humility—the ability to poke fun at oneself—to self-disdain or self-hatred. These emotions derive from our lack of confidence in Judaism. Judaism is too demanding, too difficult, too parochial, too . . . something. Jews are not strong enough; Israel is too strong. Jews look different; Jews are less attractive. In some way, our sense of being the "other" translates into feelings of inferiority.

Envisioning a community must begin from a foundation of *confidence*. Our level of financial success, political power, social acceptance, and friendliness reflected from our neighbors must be enough to allow us to take a deep breath and enjoy our transition from victim to equal. If we cannot be confident now, it is unlikely that we ever will be. If we cannot feel more positive now, we never will. Our lives are not likely to become any more secure.

Making the Choice to Choose

Our challenge now is to envision a community within the context of an America where ethnic and religious walls are permeable. As Jonathan Sarna (1994) states, "Once upon a time, most people in this country adhered to the faith and ethnicity of their parents; their cultural identity was determined largely by their *descent*. Now, religious and ethnic loyalties are more commonly matters of choice; identity, to a considerable degree, is based upon *consent*" (p. 57). Everyone—whether born Jews or Gentiles who might consider Judaism—must now *choose* to be a Jew. Born Jews may choose to be

Christian or Buddhist. Individuals who were born Jewish can choose to be nothing, to abandon their identity without converting to another religion. Those who were not born Jewish can convert to Judaism. Because of such fluidity, Judaism must become attractive to both those who are born Jews—or else they will choose to leave—*and* to those who were not born Jews, so that they will choose to join.

A logical next step, then, in our development as a successful, vibrant community in this American marketplace of ethnic and religious options is *to open the gates to all those who might choose to become Jews*. Opening the gates reverses the Jewish community's current response to the reality of American pluralism. It means abandoning a paradigm that our children and grandchildren are potential Gentiles and promoting the new belief that America is filled with potential Jews. Opening the gates means embracing *proactive conversion*, which is the open, positive, accessible, and joyful process of encouraging non-Jews to become Jews. Proactive conversion requires Jews to open the ideological and intellectual gates and help non-Jews walk through them into Jewish life. Being proactive means *encouraging* rather than *discouraging* non-Jews to consider Judaism. It involves constructing a *system* that helps non-Jews become Jews.

Proactive conversion is *not* synonymous with the aggressive recruitment that characterizes proselytizing. Should Jews be knocking on doors and trying to *persuade* random strangers to become Jews? We do not need to engage in these tactics. Opening the gates is not the same as charging out of them. It is desirable to encourage interfaith couples, children, and grandchildren of mixed families—and those non-Jews who are looking for a religious faith, for example—to consider Judaism an option. Having an open mind and heart, and offering mechanisms to acculturate those who are interested, could bring in millions without aggressively trying to coerce converts.

Certainly, advertising in newspapers about Jewish learning opportunities or public service announcements on radio, television, or the Internet are all acceptable. These are not the equivalent of proselytizing, attempting to seek out and *convince* people to be Jews. Efforts can be undertaken that simply let others know that the Jewish people welcome them and facilitate their participation in Judaism.

Even while we open the gates, however, we must have guidelines to help potential Jews become Jews. Ritual entry is an essential component in protecting the integrity of any group, so that neither individuals nor groups can make false claims about being Jews. The act of conversion requires both ceremony and an unequivocal commitment to being a Jew. The definitions of this commitment vary by denomination. Nonetheless, people are not Jews just because they say they are, any more than one is an American, a physician, or holder of a sports record just because one says so. "I feel I am a Jew, therefore I am" is not an acceptable gateway for formal admission to become part of the Jewish people. One can live as a Jew before one becomes a Jew, but a ritual conversion is essential.

Abandonment of standards is the great bogeyman in discussion of promoting conversion and inclusiveness. It is difficult for some to envision openness that is not wishy-washiness. As we open the gates, we must think about the formal steps necessary to become a Jew. Opening the gates does not mean throwing the gates so far open that we leave ourselves completely vulnerable. The music and tone, however, are as important as the words. We can adhere to standards with love and compassion.

Different Journeys, Same Destination

The pluralism of American Judaism should have something to offer the diverse explorers and seekers into Jewish life, but all denominations should live up to their own standards. They all say that they welcome sincere converts. All say that they encourage those who truly want to become Jews, that they do not treat converts differently from born Jews. Actions and deeds must match these words if proactive conversion is to flourish.

Denominational standards need to take into account the fluid and transitional nature of our real lives. Standards slip and slide, change and evolve all the time. Informing a convert about the joys of a kosher home, for example, is a positive act. A Conservative rabbi's insistence that a potential convert promise to keep a kosher home is another matter. The vast majority of Conservative Jews do not keep a kosher home. It is their choice to belong to a Conservative synagogue and not follow *kashrut*. Converts should not be made to feel that they cannot be Conservative Jews if they choose to live like most other Conservative Jews. Nor should converts feel they cannot be Reform Jews because they do want to observe *kashrut*.

The actual ritual of conversion should be uniform in the Jewish community. The multiple paths, strategies, approaches, and even tone should converge into a commonly accepted practice. The denominations continue to debate about who oversees the ritual conversion, but there should be some agreement about the ritual itself. Jewish belief does need to converge in some instances, even if only a few.

Neither is opening the gates a call to abandon the normative imperative for Jews to create Jewish families. Forming an unambiguously Jewish household is a powerful, positive event and provides a rich framework for Jewish life. The growth and vitality of the Jewish community depends on forming Jewish households and transmitting Jewish religious and cultural tradition within the family. Without such familial grounding, Judaism declines. These families are formed, however, by taking various paths.

The Jewish community cannot send a message, implicit or explicit, that a born Jew is a better Jew, a preferable marriage partner, or a more legitimate Jew. We must move away from conceiving of conversion as a stopgap measure, a last resort if a Jew cannot marry someone who was born Jewish. We must advocate conversion as an equivalent and desirable choice for the Jewish people.

Proactive conversion is not a panacea but rather one essential component of the larger process of reimagining a vibrant Jewish community and addressing the dual problems of loss of population and loss of meaning. We should be wary of seeking any magic bullet, *including* conversion. Articulating a vision, restructuring a community, restoring meaning to Jewish life for most Jews, and figuring out how to be a Jew in an open society do not lend themselves to quick fixes. Communal revitalization is confusing, takes decades to accomplish, is filled with political and social dissonance, costs billions of dollars, and requires difficult choices. Conversion is a piece—a vital piece, but still only one piece—of the puzzle. Books need to be written on how to create more Jewish families. They need to be written with a vision of a new Jewish community, written on how to rebuild Jewish communal structure. This book is specifically about how proactive conversion can do its part to revitalize Jewish life.

Actively adding to the Jewish population may seem a strange idea to many Jews. If most Jews do think about conversion, they are likely to focus on non-Jewish spouses of born Jews. Few of us contemplate really opening the gates, that is, encouraging non-Jews who do not have Jewish spouses to convert to Judaism.

Others may see the arguments in this book as superfluous or irrelevant, since they believe the gates to Judaism are already open. We say that we welcome the convert. We say that a convert is the same as a born Jew, once he or she converts. We say that rabbis are available and ready to help someone convert who really wants to become a Jew. We say that our synagogues are open to converts. Yet our language reveals emotion and thought that are far from open. Some things that we believe as a community keep the gates closed to most potential converts. What we *really* think becomes a barrier that pervades our communal structure. Most of us do not recognize how closed we really are and how much our thoughts, feelings, and actions keep people out. We need to examine what we really think, what we truly feel, what words we utter, and how we really act. We must pause and explore how we, as a Jewish community or as individual Jews, might look and sound to somebody on the outside.

Not all is grim. Signs of openness—ideological, structural, and programmatic—are becoming more common. Some of the rhetoric is changing. Some rabbis, some synagogues, and some institutions *are* proactive in helping non-Jews convert to Judaism, but they are the exception rather than the norm. Most of the Jewish communal psyche is devoted to the negative notion of preventing intermarriage, not to promoting conversion. Little is spent on promoting conversion, institutionally or programmatically. Proactive conversion is at the bottom rung of the communal ladder of priorities.

We should not dismiss or belittle the innovative activities of proactive synagogues or the creative work of some individual rabbis around the country. Good work is being done. We may be on the cusp of a new approach to conversion, but the change thus far has been painstakingly slow. We need to move ahead with much greater certainty and speed.

Our efforts should not be limited to any one approach or denomination. The Jewish community needs a wide variety of denominational, rabbinic, and structural entry points into becoming a Jew. No single set of rules, standards, structures, or procedures would be appropriate for the multitude of individual needs that potential converts and their families bring to the gates of Jewish life. Disunity among the Orthodox, Conservative, Reform, and other strands of Judaism is a plus: more entry points for more non-Jews with different attitudes and needs. Only when one group attempts to de-legitimize the others do problems arise.

To begin formulating a vision of our future, this book looks at the landscape of the Jewish community through the lens of thinking about what role conversion should play. It begins by examining where we are today and how we came to be here. It examines how our thoughts—both our unspoken fears and our institutional ideology—have led to creating communal structures and individual behaviors that keep the gates shut. It looks at the tone and attitudes of how the Jewish community speaks to the stranger who comes knocking, and it expresses our concern about what we offer the stranger when we finally unlock the gates. It concludes with recommended strategies to keep the gates open, so that we can move forward into the next Jewish civilization with strength, joy, and security.

2

How Fear Constrains Us

For many people, Jews and non-Jews alike, being afraid is intrinsic to being Jewish. For example, Rosalind was in the process of converting to Judaism. She approached her non-Jewish ex-husband, with whom she was on good terms, to discuss the impact of her impending conversion on their children. To her surprise, he gave his wholehearted support but expressed concern about antisemitism. "I live in the northeastern U.S. in a suburban area that is at least 50 percent Jewish," she wrote, "and both my ex and I grew up in Jewish neighborhoods in New York City. He [agreed] that this is a relatively easy time and place to be Jewish but wondered what might happen in the future to our children and grandchildren were political situations to shift. He noted the 60th anniversary of Kristallnacht, talked a little bit about the assimilation of German Jews prior to Hitler, and wondered how many of them might have made the same call" (e-mail to Friends of Ruth listserv, Nov. 16, 1998).

Opening the gates requires us to move beyond the constraints of being afraid of the outsider. The task is monumental, because a powerful duality fueled by fear has dominated Jewish existence for hundreds of years. On the one hand, we are afraid that our differences from others engender hostility and persecution. On the other hand, we are also afraid that we are losing the distinctiveness that separates us from others. We are afraid of the stranger, and afraid of becoming the stranger.

The stranger harms us from without, attacking randomly and wreaking annihilation. Or, the stranger enters the gates peacefully, through acceptance and affection, and overwhelms the community through gradual, benign absorption. Either way we, the Jewish people, are destroyed.

The duality of fear (see Table 2.1) works simultaneously in opposite directions. On the one hand, we fear extinction through persecution and violence because outsiders hate us. On the other hand, we fear extinction through assimilation and dissolution because outsiders accept us. We do not want to be too different yet recoil from being indistinguishable from others. We are powerless and subject to being victims, but we have too much power and visibility (in the United States or Israel) and provoke our sleeping enemies. We fear being marginalized; being unable to participate in the everyday life of the dominant culture; being excluded from schools, employment, or social settings. We worry that change destroys our traditions, and that stasis makes us unappealing to younger generations. We resist our attraction to the stranger and yet hope that the stranger will not reject us. Finally, we are petrified that there will not be enough Jews because of out-marriage—and are suspicious that there will be too many "inauthentic" Jews—if we open the gates through conversion.

Table 2.1. Duality of Fear

Fear of extinction through persecution or violence	Fear of extinction through acceptance or dissolution
Fear of being odd, different, unusual	Fear of not having a distinct identity
Fear of too much power (United States and Israel)	Fear of not enough power (United States and Israel)
Fear of too much change	Fear of being left behind
Fear of growth ("inauthentic" Jews)	Fear of stasis (not enough Jews)
Fear of the stranger	Attraction to the stranger

Contemporary Antisemitism

No matter how successful or integrated we are, most Jews still believe that antisemitism is a problem that cannot be completely eradicated. Such feelings are not irrational or paranoid. The 1997 Survey of American Jewish Opinion showed that 33 percent of those polled believe that antisemitism is currently a serious problem in the United States, and another 62 percent think it's somewhat of a problem. Only 5 percent of American Jews did not feel that antisemitism in America was a matter of concern. In response to a question regarding an increase or decrease in antisemitism over the next several years, 40 percent of the respondents believed that antisemitism would increase greatly or somewhat, 48 percent thought it would remain the same, and 9 percent believed that it would decrease somewhat or greatly. More than two-fifths of American Jews believe that some positions of influence in the United States are still closed to them.

American Jews see the potential for antisemitism to become worse than it is today. This basic perception colors all other feelings. Even among the few who believe that antisemitism has almost disappeared, most believe that wariness is essential. They hold that if antisemitism cannot be eradicated, it must be closely monitored and combated.

A collective history, both modern and premodern, influences contemporary Jews' fears. Indeed, the recounting of persecutions that we have suffered is an integral part of our liturgy and our traditional ritual observances. Formal Jewish education, which touches most of us Jews in the United States at some point in our lives, includes messages regarding the mistreatment of Jews in a variety of contexts, from Egypt through Spain and into the twentieth century. We learn about one antisemitic regime after another and about the ultimate expulsion or persecution that beset Jews in every society in which they resided.

Most first- and second-generation American Jews carry with them a different set of collective memories than those known by subsequent generations. In addition to what they have been taught, or absorbed through folklore, older Jews experienced discrimination firsthand in the United States. Some tried to pretend antisemitism did not exist, some believed it was their lot to bear, and others worked in civil rights coalitions to deal with prejudice and discrimination in general.

In the first half of the twentieth century, many Jews were foreign born. Primarily from Eastern Europe, these Jews were the victims of systematic discrimination and state-sanctioned violence. Grandparents relayed to third and fourth generations of American Jews stories of pogroms—endorsed, violent attacks on Jewish settlements. These stories, too, continue to be a part—although a fading part—of Jewish consciousness in the United States.

One should neither overstate nor minimize what the extent of antisemitism was for the first two generations of Jews in America in this century. It was different from antisemitism in Europe; the legitimacy of state-instigated violence against Jews never took root in the United States. Furthermore, Jews found themselves enfranchised in the political system in this country. Here they were able to use the electoral process to protect their individual and civil rights.

But discrimination did take place. In the first half of the twentieth century, universities had quotas on the number of Jews that could be admitted. Certain employers would not hire Jews, and positions of leadership in cultural and political circles locally and nationally were often closed to Jews. Discrimination in schools, housing, and employment were all quite real. Even though the United States was a hospitable environment for Jews, it was by no means a completely open system. The government did not promulgate antisemitic rhetoric and action, but it definitely sanctioned, and in some cases enforced, certain forms of antisemitism. For example, restrictive covenants were supported through the courts, endorsed by the Federal Housing Administration, and enforced by state governments. Until the late 1940s, the imprimatur of federal and state legitimacy was granted to segregation of neighborhoods by race and religion.

While other memories of discrimination in the United States fade, the Nazi Holocaust continues to frame all Jewish perceptions of antisemitism. A systematic destruction of Jewish life, it represents the ultimate expression of antisemitism. For Jews who lived through this time period, it remains a conscious memory; younger Jews learn Holocaust lessons. The generations of firsthand witnesses are passing away, but documentation and awareness of the Holocaust have become commonplace for younger Jews.

With the Holocaust as a grim standard, the question of Jewish safety in any society becomes salient to many Jews. Perhaps Jews are "safe" in the United States, for institutional, historical, and other reasons. Maybe another Holocaust or other form of systematic violence perpetrated against Jews is an impossibility or so remote that Jews need not be concerned about it. Nevertheless, the question itself cannot be viewed as irrelevant.

Are Jews safe in the United States? As long as democratic institutions are safe, the social and political rights of Jews are protected, along with those of other minority groups. But such stability cannot be taken for granted. Collectively, Jews are keenly aware of current, somewhat precarious, restrictions upon racial and religious discrimination. Most Jews continue to be watchful about antisemitism in the United States, wonder about how to contain it, and search for the proper social and political vehicles and alliances to protect their self-interest. Despite our social, economic, and political stature today, Jews remain a minority religious and ethnic group. In the face of this reality, most Jews remain wary.

Separation or Assimilation

American Jews have dual feelings regarding Jewish exclusiveness and exclusivity. The first is a positive view: being the chosen people carries with it a tremendous sense of specialness and unique mission, and to some degree a sense of superiority. A mythology that speaks of being a people chosen by the one and only God constitutes just about as elitist a group membership as anyone could possibly have. This elitism is reinforced by a belief system that includes bloodline, with individuals born into this covenant generation after generation. The elitism becomes extreme when bolstered by the notion that bloodline admission into the group has more legitimacy or higher standing than inclusion through conversion. The theology of being God's chosen people can provide enormous motivation to endure, accomplish, and withstand all external assaults.

We lament our terrible history of having been the victims of other peoples' political or religious wrath, but we also take tremendous pride in our endurance and ability to withstand any form of attack. Part of our cultural identity is a belief that hardship, failure, disappointment, and tragedy make a better and stronger people. No group is more adept at dealing with the misfortunes of life than the Jews. Jewish tragedy is a persistent theme in Western civilization; we are part of an ongoing saga of battling one oppressor after another.

One also can see the covenant as enormously burdensome, filled with responsibility that one may want to avoid. The feelings of being a chosen people entail fear and suspicion of the outsider, aggravated by biblical injunctions to avoid the corrupting stranger. We may feel empowered because there is no other group like us, or we may feel estranged because we must remain separate, or both.

Prevention tactics and promotion of exclusivity can lead to *withdrawal* from the general society as a means of preserving special identity. By this reasoning, Jews must remain within their own sphere, send their children to their own schools and day camps, have institutions that do not admit members of other ethnic or religious background, and, of course, marry only someone who is Jewish.

Promoting difference is a source of conflict and shame for some Jews who accept American pluralism and believe that it is wrong to claim any special place, importance, or superiority for Judaism (or any group). Jews have fully benefited from the advantages of a pluralistic society. We want to believe that everyone is equal; it gives us access and status. Racial, ethnic, and religious differences can be seen as impediments to intergroup peace and harmony. Many Jews, especially young ones, find the concept of chosenness or specialness antithetical to their belief in universalism. Therefore, for some Jews the only way to express lack of prejudice and true belief in equality is to deemphasize their own Jewishness. These people fear offending someone else. For preventionists, marrying a non-Jew is the ultimate symbol of improper interaction with the Gentile world, whereas for universalists it is the ultimate sign of safety, acceptance, and mutual respect.

One course to prevention of persecution is assimilation. For some, the cost of being different and the threat it poses to Jewish survival are so overwhelming that blending into the larger society seems safer, even if it means losing separate identity. Proponents of withdrawal strategies are willing to achieve martyrdom to maintain the status of chosen people and the unique exclusivity of Judaism; those who promote safety through an assimilation strategy, however, want to blend into the larger society and become less different than the stranger. If Jews can be more like their potential enemies, they risk less hostility from them. Indeed, this has been the creed of American Jews for generations.

The price of safety may mean losing distinctive Jewish identity. Thus others want to be safe but do not wish to lose their Jewish identity altogether. More to the point, they would like to have safety through assimilation and would be very sad to lose that separate identity, but they are not willing to trade their safety in order to be different.

Jewish communal policy is rooted in the twin desires to be like and yet unlike others, to balance uniqueness as a group and oneness with others, to feel safe from the enemy by withdrawing and to thwart potential enemies by becoming like them. Both poles seem antiquated in the context of contemporary America. They are both delusionary as well. Antisemitism is an irrational prejudice and therefore has nothing to do with how Jews actually behave. Neither groups nor individuals reduce bigotry by behaving differently, because at its source bigotry is embedded in the psyche, thoughts, and feelings of those who are prejudiced—not in the objects of their disdain or hatred.

Appropriate levels of interaction, communication, and mutual support help build bridges between Jews and other groups. This can be accomplished, however, without Jews' sacrificing our unique character. Jews can interact in ways that are distinctly Jewish and still have high levels of communication and interaction with non-Jews. Neither sameness nor withdrawal is necessary.

Beyond Fear

Transcending fear requires faith coupled with vigilance. Still, as Earl Raab (1983) describes it, some degree of wariness is a healthy sentiment toward antisemitism and is not the same as dysfunctional or crippling fear. Wariness facilitates appropriate action. Inordinate fear causes behaviors that are self-destructive. For the most part, our response to antisemitism is healthy, but our lack of a productive approach to conversion is still constrained by the debilitating influences of antisemitism.

We have developed two methods of self-protection. First, we work diligently to strengthen civil liberties, protect against dominant religious influence through government, and battle the influence of extremist groups, left or right. We embrace the principles of American democracy and pluralism; we labor, along with others, to ensure the strength of democratic institutions and protection of minorities. Any group with a history of unprotected exposure to monarchy or totalitarianism, such as the Jews have, would logically embrace this path.

In this process, we build a second appropriate social response and structure: integrating friends and allies. We are part of working coalitions in politics and business. We are major philanthropic activists in medicine, the arts, higher education, and the environment, and throughout every sector in American society. We have acculturated through our food, humor, and music. We have become essentially American, and other Americans like and respect us. In times of trouble, non-Jews do rally to support the Jews. We are not completely alone anymore.

At the same time, we have to feel secure that America is safe, that systematic discrimination is an impossibility, and that other Americans would not tolerate violence against us. Most of all, we must have faith in ourselves, and faith that we have learned our lessons. America today is not Spain in 1492 or Germany in 1933. We created the enormously effective Anti-Defamation League to fight antisemitism. We fund local community-relations councils to build intergroup relations. We support the American Israel Political Action Committee to lobby for Israel. We support elected officials. We are strong and successful. At last, we have the ability to protect ourselves with the right measure of self-reliance and strategic allies.

We must relinquish the constraints of fear in spite of history, both long past and more recent, and despite continued signs of anti-Jewish, antisemitic, and anti-Israel behavior in many parts of the world (including America). This does not imply that the battle against antisemitism is over. We still need appropriate institutions and programs to contain prejudice and ward off assaults. The goal is not to be crippled by fear, not to be foolish or entertain Pollyanna wishes that the world is free of antisemitism.

The dominant themes in Jewish life in the past sixty-five years have been linked to peril and destruction. The single largest fundraising effort in American Jewish history—was the United Jewish Appeal's Operation Exodus in the late 1980s and early 1990s. The campaign was the culmination of decades of effort to facilitate migration (to Israel and the United States) of Jews from the Soviet Union. The campaign rightfully emphasized the threat of antisemitism and repression in the Soviet Union and the latent danger continuing into the 1990s. Rescue was the motif of the campaign.

Indeed, fear has been at the heart of the great themes of Jewish consciousness in the twentieth century: *failure* to prevent disaster (the Holocaust), vigilant *battle* against disaster (Israel), and *avoidance* of disaster (Soviet Union). Today we can breathe a sigh of relief—while still maintaining our guard—and begin thinking about who and what we want to be on our terms. We must continue to deal effectively with antisemitism without being crippled by it. We can contemplate growth.

Fear of Conversion

Historically, the concept of conversion in both directions has been closely associated with antisemitism. During the Inquisition, for example, the very concept of Jews encouraging conversion would have seemed ludicrous, since Jews were being impelled to convert to Christianity to save their lives. Jews chose (or were forced) to convert away from Judaism to escape deadly persecution. Conversion has been a way out of unpleasant or dangerous existences in other societies as well. Discussions of conversion, therefore, bring up conscious or subliminal group anxiety—and sometimes terror.

Being *too* proactive about conversion to Judaism frightens us, because it is under the constant shadow of antisemitism. As far as many Jews are concerned, the pact between Jews and other religions in the United States is that we all leave each other alone. We feel that no one should attempt to coerce anyone else to adopt a religion. At the very least, such attempts are rude, disrespectful, and offensive. At their worst, they violate the boundaries of pluralism within which a thousand flowers bloom undisturbed. At the most insidious, advocacy of one religious belief or another is hateful and portends violence and destruction.

While conversion from Judaism has been an avenue for Jews to escape the burden of the group, most Jews have chosen isolation, persecution, and even death rather than abandon being the "other."

Group cohesion involves a choice to be different, to stay fundamentally estranged from the general society. Even in the absence of devotion to *kashrut*, regular synagogue worship, or other differentiating behaviors, we still remain separate by *not* practicing the dominant religion in our host culture.

As outsiders, or perhaps marginal insiders, we have often advocated social and political change. Charges of being troublemakers and subversive are often true. The idea of repairing the world carries with it the implicit assumption that the world is broken. Host cultures may bristle and sometimes erupt at the stranger in their midst who tells them that they are in need of repair. Thus we emphasize our difference just by *being*. As long as Jews are different—and vocal about our oddities—we must expect some antagonism to ensue. In America today, Jews do not have to respond to antagonism by being afraid. The need for wariness and vigilance is necessary as long as Jews are different. But we can accept its reality, do what needs to be done to keep it in check, and move on.

But what about the accustomed intensity, the survival instincts? Where do we direct all that accumulated survival anxiety and experience? Do we now channel all these emotions and energies into an obsession with assimilation? Where do we make the distinction between the amount of tension that motivates us to act positively and productively on the one hand, and on the other a level of worry and concern that is overblown and neurotic? It is hard to distinguish between the motivators that guide us and the inhibitors that keep us paralyzed.

Fear and Conversion

We are capable of heaping all of this emotional energy onto a new crisis: intermarriage. Some Jews insist we must now be as vigilant about protecting our families from non-Jewish spouses as we would in protecting them from cancer and Nazis. The family and the bloodline must be kept safe from outsiders. Even without knowing why distinctiveness is important, or what it consists of, our fear of losing it can be profound.

Even if the floodgates of intermarriage open, we can keep the psychological gates closed. The number of real Jews may diminish, but that is preferable to making conversion too easy, accepting potentially less-than-authentic Jews, intentionally watering down Judaism by believing that anyone can be a Jew.

Some argue that conversion must remain difficult, *especially* with high rates of intermarriage. The more threatened we become, the more important it is for old, exclusive standards to be enforced. The standards are like blankets we can hide under: if we cover up, the monsters will go away.

The origins of these standards—questioning potential converts, pushing them away, doubting their sincerity, demanding commitments enforced for born Jews—are based in being afraid—afraid of what the outsiders might do and afraid that embracing the stranger dilutes our uniqueness.

Arguments against conversion are most powerful when fear of external threat and internal weakness converge into one monstrous nightmare. The strangers enter our gates with malice. They feign interest in Judaism so as to take, not to contribute. The prime minister of Israel, Benjamin Netanyahu, expressed this fear most explicitly. In speaking to representatives from the Reform movement, he raised questions about "quickie conversions," by which hordes of insincere (and therefore dangerous) Gentiles enter Judaism too easily, potentially filling Israel with people who call themselves Jews but are not really ("Netanyahu Angers Reform Delegation," 1998). What will they do? Take jobs? Destroy worship? Align with the Arabs?

Prime Minister Netanyahu's fears echo the inner thoughts of some Jews. Converts bring with them non-Jewish relatives, friends, extended families. Though not having evil intent, they may have benign yet corrupting influences.

Jewish children in marriages with converts *do* have aunts and uncles called Chris and Mary who eat ham and have Christmas trees. The community responds to this situation as if Jewish children are not exposed to these influences and realities all the time. The difference is the family; it is the bulwark against the outsider. Therefore converts, even the best of them, are a danger. They bring their negative effect into the home, no matter how religious or sincere about Judaism they themselves might be. That is the best-case scenario. Worst case: they come to do harm.

Finally, the notion put forward by Jonathan Sarna (1994) and Jack Wertheimer (Wertheimer, Leibman, and Cohen, 1996)—that converts will be one-generation Jews and their children will drift off—does not have any real, empirical substantiation. Yet they argue that Jews should keep the gates closed because individuals may choose to come in whose children and grandchildren will go right back to being what they really are: non-Jews. This scenario, filled with faulty assumptions and logic, is ultimately of little importance. Suppose it is true; so what? The personal loss is real, but communal health is different. Individuals move in and out of neighborhoods; faculty come and go from universities; family members come in and out through birth, death, and divorce. An institution or a people must be strong enough to withstand, tolerate, and even encourage movement in and out; overall health and growth depend on it. Constant shifting can lead to dislocation and disruption, and too-rapid change can be destructive. Steady growth, however, can be positive. Should we keep converts out because their children do not stay? Some children of born Jews and converts *do* drift off. The goal is to keep Judaism strong and interesting enough that it does not matter if some individuals come and go. This may sound harsh, but we hope to hold most people, not all. If the community grows in spirit, form, and content, we will lose fewer.

It is unwise to let the current discussion about conversion be framed by the past. One cannot proceed into the next millennium ignoring the radical transformation of the future of Jewish life that results from the dual experiences of the Holocaust and creation of the state of Israel. Jews certainly are not ignorant of the lessons of the Holocaust. Vast migration of Jews from the former Soviet Union—largely spurred and financed by fears of potential repression and anti-semitism (at least, the worldwide campaigns to raise money to resettle them in Israel were based on these premises) and movement of Jews from Ethiopia, Syria, and elsewhere to Israel show that the Jewish populations are not waiting around for any Diaspora community to be slaughtered again. We can go to Israel if disaster is around the corner. But we must live now as full-fledged, prosperous citizens, protected by democratic institutions, free from discrimination and violence. We are free to practice our religion without repression. We should frame the questions about our religious future and how we relate to other religious groups within the context of a safe and secure America. We are equal partners, free to compete in the marketplace of American religions with all other religious groups. We can even ask others to be Jews.

3

Preventing Disaster When
We Should Be Attracting Jews

Fear makes us dwell on prevention. The mountainous landscape of confused thought regarding the future of the Jewish community generates an avalanche of strategies about prevention—meaning, keeping people from marrying non-Jews. Prevention seemingly makes conversion largely irrelevant. Most prevention efforts involve programs to build a stronger Jewish identity through formal Jewish education (such as supplemental or day schools) or informal Jewish education such as youth groups.

Most of the approaches favoring prevention are rooted in dualities that are not very useful, a collection of simplistic either-or approaches to Jewish communal life. The most prevalent one pits prevention against outreach. The former argues that building a strong Jewish identity keeps Jews from marrying non-Jews. The latter argues that Jews must do everything they can to make non-Jews feel welcome in the Jewish community. The irony, of course, is that both carry some measure of truth, yet neither is much of a community-building framework. Both views have some merit. People with stronger Jewish identities are somewhat less likely to marry people who are not born Jewish. Outreach to non-Jews is likely to bring some of them into Jewish life. These general realities, however, have little to do with comprehensive, overall strategies to build the Jewish community and seriously address maintenance of a separate Jewish identity in an open, pluralistic society.

Defensive Measures

In an article titled "Outreach to Intermarrieds: Parameters and Out-lines," Avis Miller (1993) presented the Conservative movement's three-tier strategy to "confront the challenge." Miller says that

> our first line of defense is to emphasize the mitzvah of endog-amy. We must continue to articulate that it is important for Jews to marry other Jews. . . . If, despite efforts of prevention, an intermarriage seems likely to occur, we must encourage the option of conversion to Judaism. Sincere Jews-by-choice add enthusiasm and strength to our community. They enrich us by their adult understanding of Jewish values, by their open quest for spiritual sustenance, and by their commitment to living a Jewish life. . . . Finally, if an intermarriage does occur, our third line of defense is outreach to the intermarried, in the hope that a Jewish family will result [pp. 1–2].

The contradiction in the language is startling. On the one hand, the language of prevention and defense—keeping others out—is used liberally. On the other hand, the author acknowledges that converts add a great deal to the fabric of Jewish life. If this is so, why doesn't the Conservative movement have policies that openly and actively promote conversion, not just for those who enter the realm of Judaism through the accident of marriage but also for those who are interested for their own sake? Prevention as an ideology over-shadows the benefits of conversion.

Steven Bayme (1993) echoes this language. In "Intermarriage and Communal Policy: Prevention, Conversion, and Outreach," he talks about "the intermarriage problem":

> There are at least five reasons for pursuing a policy of preven-tion. First, we do it because we must. Throughout history, no generation of Jewish leaders has ever failed to resist intermar-

riage. Therefore, no matter how unsuccessful prevention policies may prove to be, it remains our historical mandate to continue to encourage Jewish in-marriage. Moreover, were we to
abandon prevention policies, the results would be even more
disastrous. . . . Our tradition here is very clear—make no distinction between those who are born Jews and those who have
accepted the Jewish covenant. A policy that is serious about
conversion must challenge the Jewish community to adopt a
receptive and positive attitude toward converts to Judaism
[pp. 9–11].

These sentiments represent a tremendous contradiction. Using
the language of disaster, defense, prevention, and accepting conversion as a choice of last resort cannot make for an open and receptive
approach to conversion. We cannot say that marrying somebody
who was not born Jewish is terrible, and simultaneously say that once
we accept that we have such a disease we will do our best to cope
with it.

Outreach

In his monograph *Outreach to the Unaffiliated: Communal Context
and Policy Direction,* Bayme (1992) defines outreach:

Outreach may be defined as initiatives targeted to Jews far
removed from the core community and designed to effect
behavioral changes bringing the target population closer to
the communal core. Often, but not exclusively, outreach initiatives are addressed to the spiritual hunger of individuals for
transcendental meaning beyond their daily concerns and their
work and family responsibilities. Thus outreach must be differentiated sharply from adult education, which aims simply
to make Jews more knowledgeable, with no goal of effecting
behavioral changes. The ultimate success of outreach is the
baal teshuva, the adult returnee to Judaism. The term is often

used to characterize Orthodox returnees, but it should not be used exclusively in that sense. Returnees to Judaism under Conservative or Reform auspices are no less evidence of the success of outreach. As we shall see, community is a critical ingredient in successful outreach, enabling the returnee to join a warm and welcoming community of like-minded Jews, who encourage further behavioral modification through subtly (and sometimes not so subtly) expressed communal norms and standards [pp. 3–4].

He goes on to describe a number of programs—Project Link, Reform Jewish Outreach, Project Connect, Jewish community centers, and others—that attempt to connect individuals to Jewish life. All of these have the goal of building Jewish identity and connection, but none specifically deals with the intermarried or offers ways to promote conversion.

The discussion for and against outreach consists of a series of straw arguments. If outreach is defined as providing a comfortable religious home for mixed-married couples with no mission of attempting to make Jewish households, then the argument against outreach as a religious enterprise is legitimate. If, however, the goal of outreach is to create Jewish households, then the arguments revolve around strategies and tactics rather than mission. Is it better to continue to promote participation in Jewish life even for those who have already made a marriage choice but have not yet chosen to convert? Should the community make individuals who are in mixed-married households part of the Jewish community even if no conversion is intended? On a human level, efforts to help people feel comfortable through the difficult process of navigating religious differences is a worthwhile endeavor. Synagogues, Jewish family and children's services, and other institutions should help in that regard. It is not, as Bayme and others have argued, "misplaced compassion."

The Jewish community should not pursue outreach as a *singular* strategy; there is *no* single strategy. Left alone, outreach is a likely failure, but proponents of outreach do not promote it as an isolated effort. As part of a whole array of other efforts, it is helpful. If the Jewish community does better at building Jewish identity, building communal structure, and promoting conversion, the levels of success or failure for those who are mixed-married does not matter as much. Perhaps some hundreds of thousands of Jews will remain in religious limbo. But if we make progress in other realms, then the vast majority of us are part of a much stronger and vibrant Jewish community and the numbers will swell through efforts to recruit converts. We certainly can allow for the compassion of those who are unable to make choices.

Too Many of Them

Indeed, we are so concerned about mixed marriage because we fear that if patterns continue, mixed marrieds will outnumber those with a distinct and unified Jewish identity. The hysteria about the intermarriage rate topping 50 percent is the same psychology that causes Whites to move out of racially changing neighborhoods or to abandon a school system if they think there are too many Black people sending their children to a particular school. There is a tipping-point psychology: a state in which a group loses majority status and therefore fears loss of power and control. The National Jewish Population Study (NJPS; Council of Jewish Federations, 1992) was devastating because the 52 percent intermarriage rate seemed to indicate that the tipping point had already occurred. Persistent trends would produce more of *them* than of *us*. Jews were far less concerned when the intermarriage rates were 20 percent or 30 percent. The situation does not have to surpass fifty-fifty; even a 40 percent rate would still present a challenge, though not such a frightening one. The NJPS also noted that more Jews were converting *from* Judaism than *to* Judaism. The numbers were based on extremely small sample sizes and therefore are suspect, but they still add to the dismay. The tipping psychology makes prevention seem even more imperative.

Rabbi Jerome Epstein, professional leader of the Conservative movement, writes in his foreword to Alan Silverstein's book *It All Begins with a Date* (1995) of crisis and illness when discussing intermarriage: "It requires Jews to change their lives in response to the crisis created by the growing rate of intermarriage. . . . As seductive as untargeted 'outreach' and patrilineal descent might be, they simply don't 'cure' the illness we have. . . . We must spread the message to congregants of all ages—date only Jews! Marry only Jews! We must be prepared to speak out about the value of Jewish living and Jewish home life. Singles must understand and appreciate what they will be missing if they intermarry [pp. xviii–xix]." Prevention is seen as a set of barriers that must begin long before a marriage partner is even chosen.

Locking the Schoolyard Gates

A cover story of the *Jerusalem Report* titled "U.S. Jewry Pins Their Future on Education" captures the obsessive hope that building Jewish identity through education will save the Jews. In the story, J. J. Goldberg (1994) writes, "American Jewish leadership is trying to salvage the future of the community by revamping education. But the revolution is moving slowly, and it's hampered by a central unresolved question: Should teaching aim to combat intermarriage, or to bring the children of intermarried couples into the fold?" (p. 26). Both the headline and the presented strategies of what Jewish education can accomplish show the limitations and weakness of current communal thinking. The myopic focus on Jewish education reveals our lack of creative approaches to building a more vibrant Jewish community. Jewish education is what we know; it is what we pride ourselves on knowing how to do. The centrality of Jewish education is a tradition deeply embedded in our psyche and behavior. The biblical injunction to "teach your children diligently" has been inculcated throughout our culture. Relying on Jewish education to build identity, and thereby community, seems logical. As an approach to intermarriage, however, pouring resources into Jewish education is doomed to fail.

Shortsighted Vision

We tend to look backwards to what we know. The standard solution to fixing what most analysts believe is broken is a triad: Jewish education, building Jewish identity, and becoming more religious. If Jews know more, they care more. If they study more, they understand more. If they practice more rituals and return to Judaism's religious core, these together solve the intermarriage problem.

Most of what was taught, the effect it had on behavior, and the cohesiveness of the Jewish community were conceived and executed at a time when we were geographically, socially, and culturally segregated from everybody else. Jewish education was part of identity and could be used to strengthen it, but the identity also came from common language, space, history, and constraints from the outside world. A thirty-eight-year-old woman, recalling her Sunday school experiences, said, "It was the one place where I was with people like me. Just like me." In this sense, Jewish education has always been supplemental. It was an add-on, a component, not the essence of identity. A community is not only created or invigorated by teaching its members about their religion. What is learned in Sunday school or even day school must compete with baseball, MTV, the Internet, and a thousand and one other interacting or distracting ideas, recreations, and kinds of people. More knowledge, more ritual practice, a greater sense of history all are important, but they do not create peoplehood in modern America. Some people even see Jewish education as a handicap. One man we interviewed said, "All in all, I learned practically nothing. I think it's a miracle I still want to be a Jew!"

Improving the types, quality, availability, and accessibility of Jewish education should be integral to creative community-building efforts. Knowledge of Judaism, how to be a practicing member of the Jewish people in terms of ritual practice, moral and ethical guides for behavior, and establishing avenues for appropriate participation in Jewish communal life are all essential. Attention and investment in Jewish education initiatives must reinforce the merit of these activities even if the intermarriage rate were zero. How, what, and where to teach are vital but independent of how to discourage or prevent intermarriage. Pinning our hopes for communal vitality on Jewish education, especially on the system as it is currently constructed, promises to be catastrophic. In the end, such unrealizable expectations reduce support and faith in education. Knowledge is necessary to maintain the group; otherwise it becomes an empty shell. Still, this is different from Jewish education as preventive medicine.

Education Is Not Inoculation

The communal trap of too much focus on Jewish education is rooted in the supposition that intermarriage results from weak Jewish identity, or, conversely, that strong Jewish identity prevents intermarriage. It seems so logical: a strongly and positively identified Jew wants to perpetuate Jewish life, intellectually understands that Judaism is maintained through Jews marrying other Jews, and therefore makes a conscious and determined effort to marry someone who is Jewish. The logic is clean, smooth, and sensible—yet so far from the realities of the marriage patterns of most Jews. People fall in love with those with whom they work, live, go to school. Nearly all of the individuals Jews meet are not Jewish. Jewish education is not a prophylactic, inoculating Jews from Gentile encounters marked by romance and love.

Religion Is Not the (Only) Answer

Corollary to Jewish education saving the Jews is the notion that religiosity, especially ritual observance, can do so. Judaism is a religion, this argument goes, not a culture. Therefore, secularism—being just Jewish—or cultural Judaism cannot survive. This notion is almost right. Judaism without its religious components (theological or ritual) is not likely to prosper meaningfully, nor would or could this be a desirable goal. But we can consider and experience along a continuum questions of how much ritual, how much worship, how much study. Reminders that Judaism has a powerful religious component help us focus on learning how to pray, learning how to practice rituals, or learning some rudimentary or advanced theology: what is the Jewish concept of God, human relationships to God, God's commandments to each individual or to the Jews as a people? How much religiosity is necessary to maintain group identity and cohesion (and how is it measured)? Enough to provide moral and ethical guidance to the individual? Enough to make each individual feel Jewish enough to remain Jewish? Enough to teach others, including one's own children? Just enough to convince the individual to marry someone who is Jewish? Enough to make contributions to Jewish philanthropy? More? To be an authority on the Torah? How much? This series of questions is not trivial, for the religious goals may be different from the sociological ones. At the same time, religiosity must be tied to the ethnic and cultural aspects of Judaism.

Our behavior within American society shows that most Jews do not want to be isolated from other Americans in schools, jobs, friendship circles, neighborhoods, social circles, or recreation. We wish to act like other Americans in being physicians, entrepreneurs, graduate students, joggers, wine gourmets, lovers, homeowners. Religiosity has bumped, and continues to bump, up against the whole range of identities Americans cherish. Being a Jew can be a major identity, even the primary identity, but for most Jews it is not the only one. The call to religiosity, therefore, seems like a panacea, but the communal devil is in the details. What are the one or two or ten aspects of religious life that most Jews must observe to remain cohesive, experience meaning, and distinguish Jews from others? Which of these can most logically fit into the multiple identities of American Jews? How does Jewish education fit into this cohesiveness?

Do we really believe that the attractiveness of alternatives of all kinds—food, ideas, places to visit, experiences to explore, and so on—ceases to tempt and attract individuals once they know more about Jewish history and Talmud? Maybe. For some. Building Jewish education *can* lead to a stronger Jewish identity; focusing more on religiosity can be part of a cohesive strategy to build the Jewish community. But thinking that Jewish education will save the Jews rests on a fantasy that we are in a different century and a different country. Quality Jewish education is necessary, but not sufficient.

A Mixed Bag of Books

The flaw of placing too much emphasis on Jewish education has to do with the enterprise itself. Education that is designed to aid learning about Judaism, on the one hand, and education that builds a strong instinctual love for Judaism on the other have different thrusts. Most of the system currently in place does not accomplish either. Some of the advocacy for Jewish education is partly gratuitous institutional positioning; some is righteous, sincere, and honest belief in the current system. Both kinds of advocates lay claim to communal resources for institutions, synagogues, day schools, Jewish community centers, and others.

Some of the programs are worthwhile, some are not. Some are effective, and some are not. If we really want to optimize the effect of Jewish education, we are not likely to do so within the institutional framework as it is currently constructed, with teaching what is taught, and with the personnel we have. Some of our Jewish educational system is good. There are some excellent schools, some outstanding teachers, some fine Jewish camps, some wonderful trips to Israel. Most of the resources that are currently expended, however, end up in a black hole of mediocrity. Demanding more Jewish education could be more of the same.

The success stories are less abundant than they must be to achieve communal growth. The Jewish educational system is not stagnant; it is just not moving quickly or systematically enough to achieve the degree of change necessary to build a visionary Jewish community, and more money alone does not solve complex systemic problems.

Anyway, Jewish education cannot save the Jews without a vision of the future. Jewish educational ideology rooted in fear is sure to fail. The idea of building enough identity to ward off a non-Jewish mate is cemented in the old paradigm of fear and is unappealing to younger generations of Jews. Is this what Jewish schools are supposed to do? J. J. Goldberg (1994) writes, "In other words, the body of organized Jewry may be willing to boost its spending on Jewish education, and the spirit of reform may be strong. But the community hasn't agreed on what kind of Jewish future the schools are supposed to build—or whether schools can do the job at all" (p. 31). They cannot do the job if the goal is prevention.

Strategies for Learning

What is accomplished depends on how much the community is educating for the sake of *knowledge* and how much for the sake of *transmitting identity*. These are two goals that can be intertwined, but they use different techniques, institutional venues, and personnel. Strategies to educate about Judaism may be quite different from strategies to mold Jewish identity. It may be that most of the emphasis at an early age should be on identity, with acquisition of knowledge to come later. For example, Jewish summer camps and trips to Israel produce strong visceral and positive feelings about being Jewish. Day schools provide much more knowledge of the history and practice of Judaism. Both kinds of opportunities reinforce the creation of Jewish peer groups. College campuses may be an ideal venue for learning about Judaism compared to other religions. However, neither accumulating knowledge nor transmitting identity should be driven by the belief that the primary benefit of these efforts is that Jews will not marry non-Jews.

American culture thrives on the new and the different, experimentation and change. American Jews are exactly that: Americans first, Jews second. Even if we were Jewish Americans, such that the American component were secondary, it still would constitute a phenomenally powerful influence. Proponents of building Jewish identity somehow believe that strong enough identity can withstand all the assaults and allures of competing cultures and philosophies. This may be so. But the vehicles for successful integration of competing cultures and ideas are not likely to be what somebody learned at age ten in a supplemental school, or even at age sixteen in day school. These are helpful building blocks, but the task must be completed throughout one's lifetime. The Jewish organizational and institutional structure is not equipped to handle identity formation and reinforcement for individuals who are beyond college, or unmarried, or disaffiliated. This is a combination of forces characterizing many people in their twenties and thirties.

A significant proportion of Jews with many years of Jewish education and a strong sense of self as Jew is still going to marry non-Jews. The probability that someone with a more intensive Jewish background marries another Jew is considerably higher than for someone without such background. This tautology must be examined for what it really is. Those who receive more Jewish education participate in more Jewish activities and are likely to be more highly associated with the community of Jews than those who receive less Jewish education or none. Sending children to a Jewish day school may either reflect a certain level of communal involvement or lead to it. The education itself is probably less important than the network it represents or tends to build. Sending a child to Israel may have a life-changing effect on a Jewish teen in terms of strengthening his or her positive feelings about being a Jew. The same may be said for a mission to Israel for an adult. Yet all of these positive feelings are minimized without a strong community network in which to express them. The task of building Jewish *community* is separate and distinct from the task of building Jewish *identity*. A Jewish community bereft of strong identity is shallow and ultimately cannot sustain itself. On the other hand, building Jewish identity without simultaneously building communal structures in which to express that Jewish identity does not succeed in America's open society. The walls between religious, racial, and ethnic groups in America are far too permeable to believe that a strong sense of religious or ethnic identity provides some definitive prevention of intermarriage.

Prevention Does Not Lead to Growth

Finally, preventing intermarriage is not the prerequisite for Jewish vitality. Growth is essential and does not come from prevention tactics. Growth comes from encouraging growth. The Jewish community collectively understands that the population is shrinking in size. We understand that most Jews live Jewish lives that transmit little to each successive generation, intermarried or not. Most of us do not know enough about being Jewish or do enough that is Jewish to encourage our children or grandchildren to be meaningfully Jewish so as to make more generations of Jews. This is a real problem we need to address. The focus on preventing intermarriage saps our creative energy and resources from imagining what Judaism can be, and from developing new social, cultural, and religious structures and processes to make it happen. Prevention does just that: it *prevents* us from creating a better Jewish community. It is nonsense to say that the Jewish community is doing just fine. It is just as nonsensical to believe that the problem is intermarriage.

Still, we continue to search desperately for the magic solution, the silver bullet to kill the intermarriage werewolf. One pronouncement after another declares that an institutional or programmatic initiative will save the Jews. Pick the Jewish communal revelation of the day—Jewish camps, adult education, day schools, synagogue transformation. Each new or old postulate moves around limited programmatic and institutional lines, but the promise is always the same: *this* program will do the trick.

Buyer beware. The solutions come and go like diet fads. They are facile answers guaranteed to propel the Jewish community someplace quickly and completely. There is no silver bullet, however, and there is no quick fix. Redesigning the Jewish community requires a multitiered strategy, and it takes a long time, many new ideas, and a great deal of money.

The prevention approaches to intermarriage are boring. They reveal an institutional recalcitrance that is rooted in self-serving double-talk. The aim is to maintain the current institutional structure. We will not recapture the Jewish community of the 1950s (or that of the 1850s). The 1990s are rapidly turning into the twenty-first century. We do need to invest in the best activities, to learn more about being Jewish. Jewish education, though, will not save us, nor will prevention. Rebuilding the Jewish community—fundamental change—saves us. Advocacy for conversion does not solve all of our problems (although it helps). Still, the ideological barriers to conversion are enormous.

4

Why We Believe What
We Do About Conversion

There are ideological and emotional barriers to proactive conversion that lead to the building of structural walls. How we think and feel keeps people out, and this translates into what we do and into the institutions we construct to carry out our ideological and emotional wills. Many of our reactions to conversion have legitimate origins, based in realities that made sense in other places or prior times. Do they make sense in contemporary America? For the most part, they do not.

The most prevalent intellectual and emotional reaction to conversion is simultaneously theological, historical, and sociological: one either is or is not a Jew. A person is inside or outside—not in-between.

Jews are part of a covenant with one God that excludes worship of other gods and participation in other religions. By definition, one cannot be a Jew *and* practice another religion. Therefore, the concept of conversion is linked to absoluteness, and it makes us feel and act rigidly.

Old Habits, New Thoughts

Old beliefs make us feel secure because they are familiar, even if they are no longer pertinent or useful. Any change requires leaving something behind. That which is transformed is no longer. Leaving behind feels like loss, no matter if what is abandoned is bad or good, positive or negative. An open-conversion ideology makes Jews feel many kinds of loss: personal, familial, institutional, and communal.

We do not even have good ways to discuss conversion. If someone who converts is a full Jew, then he or she should no longer be a convert, or different from a born Jew. Indeed, the distinction that is embedded in the supremacy of the bloodline contradicts the outcomes of conversion. Lawrence Epstein (1995) points out that we need a different language to discuss more open and fluid access to Jewish life:

> Because the subject of conversion to Judaism is fraught with so much controversy, let me note some points here. The first problem is language. As I have noted elsewhere, there is no appropriate, Jewish way to discuss those who have embraced Judaism. They are simply Jewish. Their status should not be considered as somehow separate from other Jews by this discussion of their religious quest. Some people who have become Jewish do not like the word *convert*, thinking it sounds un-Jewish or having some other objection. The other terms, such as *Jew by choice, choosing Jew, proselyte, new Jew*, and so on, are used at some places in the anthology. We don't have a clear, good language in English to discuss those who join the Jewish people. I hope those who do not like the word *convert* will forgive its usage; I employ it because it is linguistically the simplest term and the one most widely understood [pp. xii–xiii].

Part of the emotional opposition to conversion is habitual. It is what Jews are used to feeling. Scrutiny of these feelings is difficult to launch—as is dealing with any habits, good or bad. Habits can evolve into tradition, and tradition is the life blood of Judaism. Barriers to conversion have been constructed over and over again; opposition to conversion has been codified. Tradition can be a powerful cover for a bad habit. Questioning the sincerity of the potential convert, for example, falls into this category.

Lack of understanding of what is new constitutes a high emotional barrier. How do Jews conceive of something to do that they do not understand experientially? Thinking about proactive conversion involves imagination, which can evoke negative as well as positive images: we can see rainbows or monsters. Inventing a future and working toward it are difficult.

Jewish imagination is also limited by what other religious groups do. Therefore, thinking about proactive conversion quickly translates or deteriorates into scenes of Jehovah's Witnesses knocking on the door, or television evangelism. The Jewish tradition of conversion is too far in the past to be relevant, even though Jews have successfully promoted conversion in other eras and in other places. Our inability to imagine futures that are not an imitation of what we disapprove of or deem inappropriate limits our capacity to rethink conversion.

Clinging to the past keeps us burdened by a worldview that asks, "Why would anybody *want* to be Jewish?" Our history of discrimination logically leads us to escape from our Jewish identity, not to ask others to join. The philosophies and institutions that support conversion could not possibly have developed in the European context, or even in the United States before now. They would have been impossible to construct. But they can develop now within high levels of security and freedom.

First, we have to become comfortable with the idea that Judaism is an attractive, legitimate religious option for individuals of all faiths to consider. We are historically unconditioned to this idea and therefore wary of its radical dimensions and uncharted consequences. Even if some of our institutions need retooling and our communal structure needs reviving, Judaism is wonderfully alive.

We must also deal with our desire to remain special. We may loathe our exclusivity and separateness on the one hand, but we crave it and are proud of it on the other. Therefore, the notion that anybody can be Jewish seems to trivialize our specialness and suggest that Judaism is not unique after all. As long as Judaism is attained through birthright, distinctiveness is preserved. Limited access ensures its special character. Arguments for discouraging conversion and concentrating on the core of committed Jews reinforce the sense of exclusivity and specialness. After all, is it not better to have three million legitimate, serious Jews than a community of ten million inauthentic Jews or interlopers into the faith?

We take pride in our accomplishments in education, art, science, and politics. We promote our martyrdom as part of our group cohesion and are also proud that we have endured. We do not wish to share this unique historical experience with just anybody. The desire to keep the other out is strong because the limits of exclusion guarantee a special place for us.

Keeping converts out is therefore flavored with a component of collective martyrdom: we have suffered so much as a people that strangers should not be able to call themselves Jews without having paid the historical price of suffering. Horrible persecutions carry with them a badge of honor. Ancestral triumph over enemies and the litany of success in outlasting history's villains are a source of enormous pride to us. The incalculable price we have paid to remain Jewish prevents us from sharing our identity too freely. Non-Jews have no right to share in this history.

Another element prohibits us from actively promoting our religion to others: most of us consider ourselves to be ethnic, secular, or cultural Jews, as opposed to religious Jews. Even if we believe that we are religious, we do not believe we are religious enough. For those who consider themselves cultural Jews and who hold that Judaism is primarily ethnic, the idea of welcoming others through the religious door seems counterintuitive. Active conversion to a Judaism that is defined ethnically and culturally seems anathema to those who cannot see themselves in religious terms. The attempt to convert others to one's faith is largely dependent on the strength and conviction of one's own religious behavior (which is nonexistent for some and marginal for most). Many Jews believe they cannot possibly help others convert because Judaism is defined by, say, the tastes or smells of childhood—an acculturation process that comes through generations and a sense of belonging that has little or nothing to do with religious doctrine or practice. To some extent these feelings are real and must be addressed. Acculturation does take place over time, and it must be nurtured. Non-Jews can inculcate ethnic and cultural Judaism, but not all at once.

An individual who lives among Jews and adopts the folklore patterns of the group is sometimes seen as "more Jewish" than someone who was born Jewish. Jews understand that this metamorphosis can take place, but not necessarily as a result of adopting religious principles at the outset. Because Judaism is a way of life as well as a set of religious beliefs and practices, the conversion process is sacred in both religious and communal terms. The rites of passage, therefore, are made to be a difficult initiation (rather than an adoption of faith, which can give immediate entree into the group). The barriers to conversion sometimes have much more to do with ethnic and communal purism and cultural and secular protectionism than they do with theology. *Halachic* objections, therefore, should be seen for what they are: less an adherence to Torah imperative and more a way to keep strangers out of the Jewish peoplehood.

This creates enormous dissonance for contemporary Jews who pride themselves on their liberal beliefs and their rigorous championing of an open and tolerant society of racial, ethnic, and religious equality. Reform and Conservative Jews especially do not wish to admit that they carry any form of prejudice or bigotry, knowing fully that Judaism can be achieved through conversion as well as birthright but feeling in their heart of hearts, perhaps, that birthright is more complete.

Opposition to open conversion is also denial or reluctance to admit that societal walls are permeable. If individuals can easily convert to Judaism, the opposite is also the case. If we acknowledge that Judaism is open to anyone who chooses to be a Jew, then the corollary is obvious: that any Jew can opt for another religion. Emphasizing religiosity over ethnicity raises suspicions about whether these advocates really mean what they say. By reemphasizing Judaism as a religion only, the gates are open for Jews to opt out more readily if they no longer believe in God; belong to a synagogue; or have much attachment to worship, spiritual matters, or religious beliefs.

Judaism as a peoplehood welcomes the involvement of those who volunteer and fund Jewish organizations and agencies, are involved in Jewish peer groups, and so on, even if they do not consider themselves religious. The peoplehood emphasis encompasses all. Until recently, ethnic ties seemed to suffice; lack of religious participation did not seem much of a detriment to group survival. The call for increased religiosity is based on the hope that participation in religious life also strengthens communal ties.

Welcoming non-Jews through the religious door may strengthen the religious component of Judaism, but it then weakens the communal and ethnic components. This vast array of contradictions paralyzes our community. It prohibits formulating any cohesive thoughts about how to strengthen both ethnic and religious components of the community. It also stops us from rethinking which elements from each part of our community we should build on to strengthen the core of Jewish peoplehood. Greater emphasis on religiosity opens the door to anyone who chooses to practice Judaism as a religion. These individuals can in turn bring great vibrancy to the ethnic group, as long as the mechanisms for acculturation and identity formation remain strong.

Perhaps the greatest fear among those who wish to keep out the stranger is that the ethnic and communal ties are too weak to assist in-group inculcation and value formation. Just as some Jews believe they are not religious enough, others may believe the community is not strong enough, distinct enough, or separate enough to absorb newcomers. Perhaps the community has become too weakened to identify the aspects of peoplehood that converts, through both the religious and ethnic doors, would adopt.

Asking people to choose Judaism requires more of a sense of which identity and which behavior people are being asked to assume. Jews cannot advocate others' joining their ranks without offering a set of values and norms. The mistake that is often made, however, of putting forward primarily rules and regulations about ritual observance, including synagogue attendance, Shabbat, and perhaps even rudimentary theology. The other elements of Jewish identity are treated with much less importance. A convert must assume an ethnic identity, a culture, a people, and a nation, which for many Jews are just as important—and sometimes more important—than the religious aspects. The question is one of multiple layers and of emphasis. The religious appeal may be effective with certain personality types, within certain households or family constellations, or with some people having a particular family or personal history. Yet other types may be attracted to the cultural aspects of Judaism, and still others by the historical or peoplehood aspects of Judaism. All of these cannot be expected to be learned quickly, or necessarily before formal commitment to conversion.

More often than not, neither a potential spouse nor a random acquaintance feels knowledgeable or comfortable enough to explain his or her own Judaism, much less promote Judaism to others. This is not aberrational or endemic to Jews alone. Many racial, ethnic, and religious groups struggle with their identities, and with defining their norms and values and explaining themselves to the outside world. Any individual might be hard pressed to explain the meaning of being White, the history of the Episcopal church, the basic tenets of American culture, or the history of Catholicism in America. Much may be assumed or intuited, practiced or observed, and much may be difficult to define or articulate for any particular individual. The complexity of Judaism makes this effort even more problematic. There is no catechism; the religious laws are characterized by millennia of interpretation and reinterpretation. Jews have been scattered as a people through scores of nations and have been periodically estranged by custom, language, and beliefs. Since

Judaism has been and is a religion, culture, people, and nation, one may choose to offer any or all of these as explanations of what it means to be a Jew.

Lack of knowledge of Judaism in any of its forms can be embarrassing and severely limiting in attempting to encourage converts. Jewish individuals may recoil from their own lack of knowledge and the feelings of insecurity this ignorance engenders. We may become embarrassed when speaking to someone who is not Jewish who is probing about the purpose, meaning, and definitions of Jewish life. It is not impossible for us to say we do not care, rather than that we do not know, when presented with difficult questions about Judaism.

Familial Barriers

No ideological barrier is as high as the one erected by the potential convert's new Jewish spouse, in-laws, or other family members. Interfaith marriages should be one focus of conversion efforts. Yet it is often the Jewish spouse who stands in the way of the non-Jew's journey toward Judaism.

The Jewish spouse may be a passive or an active barrier. Passively, the Jewish spouse simply does not act to move the non-Jewish partner toward Judaism. Either Judaism is not important to the born Jew, or the Jewish partner views Judaism and Jewishness as too burdensome, too dangerous, too boring. These attitudes translate into avoidance behaviors. The Jewish partner may not talk about being Jewish, or may talk about it with the kind of cynicism that barely disguises shame and a sense of inferiority about being other in the company of the non-Jewish spouse. Certainly the Jewish partner does not ask the non-Jewish partner to learn about Judaism, let alone to convert.

Creating a Jewish family because of marriage is often the primary motivation for non-Jewish spouses to explore conversion. For many Jewish spouses, a Jewish household is enough. Why bother for the non-Jewish partner to convert?

For example, Jackie's husband "would never have said that he wanted me to [convert] or asked me to. We had an agreement that when we had children we would raise the children Jewishly. I made the decision to explore Judaism so that I wouldn't be a passive participant in our Jewish family life." Her exploration led her to discover a spirituality missing since her childhood as a practicing Episcopalian.

Although she has not yet converted, Jackie plans to attend services with another Jew-by-choice and to take their (already converted) daughter once she is old enough. Her husband will not attend services with them. He "makes a joke that he hopes I never become religious. He is fifty years old, he is comfortable with how he is Jewish, and doesn't want anything new. He was missing the Jewish family home, and now he has it."

Although he strongly identifies as a Jew, Jackie's husband has actively prevented Jackie from practicing the kind of Judaism that she finds most meaningful. "Last year I wanted to go to High Holy Days and I went to get tickets, [but] when it came to going, we never went. He kept saying, we'll go in an hour, we'll go in an hour. And the holidays came and went and we never went anywhere, so this year I didn't even bother."

Threatening the Family

When a non-Jewish partner ignores family barriers and decides to approach Judaism anyway (for any of a number of reasons: because of a desire to raise children in one religion, because the Jewish in-laws expose the non-Jew to Judaism, because Judaism is appealing, and so on), the Jewish partner may perceive the move as a threat.

Barbara found that her decision to explore Judaism did not please her Jewish husband: "My husband married this former Christian because a Jewish household wasn't important enough to him at the time. It was frightening to him when I announced my intentions to convert. We had been married five years and had two children. His greatest fear was that he would come home to see some 'black hats' blow-torching the oven to make it kosher" (e-mail to Friends of Ruth listserv, Sept. 22, 1998).

The threat when a non-Jewish partner journeys toward Judaism can be the threat of *exposure*—of the Jewish partner's lack of knowledge about Judaism or lack of religious commitment. Conversion is a religious process; many born Jews see Jews-by-choice as being "better Jews" for their religious observance and knowledge, even if they themselves have no desire to adopt the religious practices of their spouses.

Anne's husband is "not religious at all, doesn't go to services. He is supportive and accepting of my wish to convert, but he is sometimes afraid that I may become 'some kind of nut' and go overboard with 'the religious stuff'" (e-mail to Friends of Ruth listserv, Sept. 19, 1998). Again, conversion, as it is currently constructed in the Jewish institutional world, is a religious process; how can Anne convert to Judaism and avoid the "religious stuff"? How can a Jewish spouse be "supportive and accepting" and still place limits on the amount of Jewishness that comes into the home or into their lives?

Even if the Jewish partner is strongly identified as a Jew, a non-Jewish spouse's transformation can represent a threat. For some born Jews, Judaism is a primary defining characteristic, one to which they would like to retain exclusive rights. The choice to marry a non-Jew, in fact, may be a choice to bridge both worlds, the Jewish and the non-Jewish; the conversion of a non-Jewish spouse is a bomb that threatens to destroy the bridge.

Sylvia's husband had an "image of himself as this incredible Jew, but it was his own definition of *his* family, *his* identity." They had a Jewish household, were members of a congregation, and enrolled their children in Jewish day school. Sylvia was, by her own description, "a good Jew," although she had not converted. At the suggestion of their rabbi, who told her that their children would not be allowed to become a *bar* or *bat mitzvah*, she decided to complete the process and formally convert. "As I became more and more Jewish, it was not positive for [my husband]. I was interested in progress, in learning more, and it was a bad thing for our marriage." They eventually divorced, and Sylvia later married another Jewish man and set up a Jewish household.

The Jewish spouse is not the only family barrier. Sometimes Jewish in-laws reject non-Jewish spouses, even if they convert, because in their heart of hearts Jews-by-choice can never be "real Jews" (and by extension, any grandchildren are "not really Jewish"). This is the "blood is better" sentiment. Prior to her conversion, Sylvia's father-in-law made it clear that she would never be accepted into the family. When Sylvia was pregnant with their first child, her father-in-law rebuffed her. "He said, 'I won't hold a *goyishe* grandbaby.' I was so angry to be rejected. I didn't convert until after he died."

The Direct Case Against Conversion

Jews Do Not Proselytize

Generally, one or more of six reasons are given for opposing active conversion in the Jewish community. The first is simple and straightforward: Jews don't do that. Individuals argue that there is no tradition of proselytizing in Judaism and that Jews have always discouraged converts. Many people believe it is simply not a Jewish thing to do; it is outside the realm of their experience and not part of what they believe to be our religious or cultural tradition. *Other* groups proselytize; it is something that the Jehovah's Witnesses or Mormons do, but not Jews. In some sense, it is another way for us to claim separate and distinct identity. We often like to distinguish ourselves not only by what we do as a religious group but also by what we do not do. Proselytizing and encouraging conversion are for the *goyim*, or at least that is how we see it today in America. That Jews have promoted conversion at different times in the past is unknown to most Jews.

It's the Law

A second argument is one of law, from the Torah and its interpretation. Opponents of proactive conversion argue that the tradition of opposition to conversion comes from Jewish law; they cite chapter and verse of commands for endogamous marriage or opposition to mixed marriage. They argue that the Jewish reluctance to encourage conversion comes not from historical and sociological pressures from the external Christian and Muslim environment not to do so but rather from internal legal opposition that can be found in the Torah, the prophets, and elsewhere.

Rabbi Moshe Greenberg (1996) traces some of the history and theological underpinnings of negative attention toward Gentiles. A reverse rejection has developed; as Greenberg states: "A long line of Jewish tradition is imbued with this haughtiness toward gentiles. . . . It is the bad fruit of the concept of election, animated by a good dose of hostility toward the gentiles because of the fathomless suffering they have inflicted on Jews. It also deals a moral victory to the Jew who was bereft of means to defend himself other than with words" (p. 32).

These traditions are entwined with injunctions not to take non-Jewish wives and to avoid too much contact with Gentiles in general to prevent adopting their godless customs. We have felt the need to preserve our distinctiveness and to protect ourselves by separation.

When Harold Schulweis, a prominent Conservative rabbi, wrote about the need to promote conversion, he experienced a torrent of negative responses. In a letter to *Moment* magazine (August 1997) responding to Schulweis's call to seek converts, one adversary wrote:

I am amazed that Harold Schulweis expects *Moment's* enlightened readers to accept his equating of 1990s proselytizing with the conversion of Ruth the Moabite. Even the slightly informed student of *Tanach* knows that Ruth was rebuffed several times in her quest to embrace the God of Naomi. In fact, it is from the story of Ruth that our rabbis follow the practice of turning away the prospective convert three times prior to acceptance of the non-Jew into a conversion program. There is more than a semantic difference between "seeking" converts and "converting seekers. . . ." Jews by choice, welcome; Jews by recruitment . . . ? Why not begin by recruiting the over 50 percent unaffiliated members of our own religion before we chase the world? [pp. 19–20].

Yet there is serious disagreement about how the proselyte is to be viewed through *Halacha* (as in most matters!). Some call it a curse, some a blessing, some say we are compelled to do it, and some say we must not.[1]

Another letter writer responded to Schulweis by arguing that Jews are a race:

Schulweis errs when he waves off the issue of "genes and chromosomes." In fact, the Jewish people are a "race." . . . Studies prove Ashkenazi and Sephardic Jews are of the same racial stock. The retention of Jewish ethnicity in 2,000 years of exile is a remarkable accomplishment. . . . Many Jews support maintaining the ethnicity of Eskimos, American Indians and African Americans, yet label as "racist" Jews who hold the same ideas about our own community. In order to boost falling demographics, they urge massive conversion, despite the reality that the acceptance of large numbers of converts would be non-violent racial genocide. What Hitler attempted with violence would be accomplished in a type of collective suicide, the end of Jewry as an ethnic body. . . . Rather than seeking converts, responsible Jewish leaders should enforce a ban on all conversions. Religious schism, ethnic destruction, social chaos, all this and more, are the fruits of contemporary conversions. Indeed, conversion is not a solution but a modern-day golden calf. Like the golden calf of old, it has the potential for our self-destruction as a people [*Moment*, Aug. 1997, pp. 17–18].

In an August 1996 article in *Moment*, Ellen Jaffe-Gill, author of *Embracing the Stranger: Intermarriage and the Future of the American Jewish Community* (McClain, 1995), writes a scathing description of the Jewish community's approach to converts and the conversion process:

> Ask most congregational rabbis about converts to Judaism, and they'll reel off lists of dedicated individuals serving the temple as committee chairs, officers, and Torah readers. Talk to a Jewish in-law of a convert, and you're likely to get an earful about "the best Jew in the family": how beautifully and diligently she makes Shabbat, or how he inspired the whole family to learn more about Jewish history. Drop in on an Introduction to Judaism class, and you'll see a room dotted with prospective Jews aglow with the conviction that their journey represents a spiritual homecoming. Yet ask many "biological" Jews how they view converts and they'll describe them with the same regard Pat Buchanan has for immigrants: they're everywhere, and they're not doing us any good [McClain, 1996, p. 30].

Live and Let Live

The third opposition comes from those who are worried that active conversion produces a backlash in the Christian community. Some involved in intergroup relations believe that Jews have worked very hard to reach accommodations with the Catholic church and other religious faith traditions to respect the integrity of our religion and not to seek us out for conversion. These were hard-fought battles, and quite necessary because efforts to convert Jews have often been tied to persecution and violence. Conversion of Jews was not a benign undertaking. Some people argue that we do not attempt to convert Christians, and therefore Christians should not attempt to convert us. Some Jews believe that America lets all religious faiths bloom in peace and everyone should leave everyone else alone. Those who fought this battle are concerned that we would be reneging on our implicit commitment.

For those who see progress in containing antisemitism as a series of victories in a long war that has not yet been won, open conversion seems a dangerous tactic in a still very hostile world. Some Jews believe that an aggressive Jewish stance in the religious marketplace either produces antisemitism or unleashes latent antisemitism. Simply put, many Jews are afraid to stir up what they believe would be a tremendous hornet's nest and that they must leave well enough alone.

There is also fear that such action would open the way for Christian groups to proselytize among Jews. These activities are clearly a reality anyway. Jews for Jesus, for example, is a clever means of recruiting Jews to Christianity. Furthermore, television and radio as well as other media are filled with aggressive attempts to convert any member of any religion to Christianity, including Jews. Just because Jews are not specifically targeted for conversion does not mean we are not actively and aggressively exposed to conversion attempts. Jehovah's Witnesses, for example, proselytize door-to-door, indifferent to the religious identities of those who are in those households.

Indeed, the Southern Baptist reaffirmation to proselytize actively among Jews created some alarm. To some observers, it sounded like traditional antisemitism or worse: "The Southern Baptist move has enraged American Jewish leaders, who call it an insult and a major setback for interfaith relations. Abraham Foxman, the national director of the Anti-Defamation League, says the church's two-year-old effort to convert Jews reminds him of the Holocaust and calls it 'an affront to the memory of those who were murdered by intolerance'" (San Francisco Chronicle, June 9, 1998, p. 44).

Why specifically target Jews for Christian conversion? Has the world not seen enough horrific attempts by dominant Christian cultures to "save" the Jews? The call of the Southern Baptists seems ugly, a recidivist campaign not worthy of contemporary acceptance. We cannot ignore the past.

But is such a campaign antisemitic? That could be its intent. Abe Foxman should raise the question. We must keep one another honest in these endeavors. Rules need to be devised and followed. But imagine for a moment a sincere and legitimate effort among Southern Baptists to bring Jews into their religious faith tradition. They undertake this process with good will, openness, and an honest set of limits; asking, promoting, and offering are all acceptable, but coercing, threatening, forcing, and denigrating are not. Suggesting that Jews are destined for hell, for example, immediately crosses the line. At the same time, imagine that Jewish organizations decide to do the same: to target Southern Baptists for conversion to Judaism. Same rules, same goals, same positive intent. It is possible that some Jews would convert to become Southern Baptists. It is even more likely, since most Jews do not choose to become something else, that an equal or greater number of Southern Baptists would choose to become Jews.

The need to avoid the appearance of proselytizing has increased our shyness about promoting conversion, even when we believe it is legitimate. In an article in the *St. Louis Post-Dispatch* about bringing unaffiliated Jews closer to Judaism, Dru Greenwood, director of the Reform movement's outreach department, is quoted as saying: "Perhaps, in our eagerness to avoid the appearance of proselytizing, we have been too reticent in suggesting the possibility of conversion to the non-Jews among us. We need to find a middle ground between badgering and avoidance, where we can sensitively invite the choice of Judaism" (Cornell, 1991, p. 10A).

Other religious faith traditions in America promote conversion safely within the American religious landscape. If we have truly reached equal religious equality, then we too have the right to engage in this activity. Opposing conversion on the grounds that it evokes the specter of antisemitism is not an insane argument; it is one that has to be put behind us if we are to move on to the next phase of our civilization.

First Things First

The fourth argument for opposing active conversion is that we should undertake other communal efforts first. This, of course, is part of the argument for working on the core versus the margin, concentrating on those who are the most logical targets for commitment before we deal with others. This is a spurious argument. There is no evidence that concentrating on the core produces a stronger and more vibrant Jewish community. Those most involved become somewhat more so if they receive the bulk of communal attention. It is unknown, however, whether one million new Jews through conversion or five million makes a better and stronger Jewish community, because such an endeavor has never been attempted in modern times. The debate always focuses only on Jews who are already involved or uninvolved within the Jewish community. These arguments have more to do with efforts that are comfortable and simple to execute than assessing long-term effects. Risk avoidance dominates, with institutions wanting to rely on what they believe is tried and true.

The risk of failure is daunting. Leaders of Jewish institutions, both lay and professional, do not want to squander precious political and financial assets on programs that may or may not work, or on populations that seem hard to reach. Concentrating on the core of those who are already highly committed, or at least committed enough that the organizations and institutions feel their involvement can be heightened, seems like a safe and secure strategy to pursue. If marginal Jews seem risky, non-Jews seem totally out of reach. The first-tier approach, which can last a long time, constitutes a great delaying tactic to dismiss other populations without having to bother with them.

Most important, who decides to write off whom? Who should be included or excluded? What measures do we use to decide who is core and who is marginal? Who is anointed to identify the good and salvageable Jews?

Futility

The fifth argument against open conversion is that it does not work. The proponents of this view believe there are not enough people outside the Jewish community who may be interested in Judaism, or that the most marginal Jews will never be interested in Judaism, so why bother with non-Jews? The won't-work argument is often tautological in nature. Some analysts argue that we have not been able to convert those within our mixed-married ranks, so why would the community be able to convert more non-Jews through outreach efforts? The glaring flaw of this argument, of course, is that the Jewish community has paid very little attention to helping people convert. Since Jewish organizations and institutions do not promote conversion, how would we know if such efforts were fruitful or not?

Steven Bayme (1993), director of the American Jewish Committee's Communal Affairs Department, argues that conversionary policies have little effect since so few individuals currently convert in the milieu of pluralism. Bayme's statement that there are few who convert and therefore we should spend little effort on conversion is the tautology in which the Jewish community finds itself caught as the twentieth century ends. Few people convert because the Jewish community makes it so difficult and has practically no institutional apparatus to make conversion possible. Bayme's argument is a self-fulfilling prophecy. The system is structured to oppose conversion and make it difficult. Therefore, "it won't work because it hasn't worked" relies on evidence of intentional efforts to keep it from working—and it preserves a status quo that is hostile to conversion.

It is true that efforts of proactive conversion do not work in the system as it is currently constructed. That is why we must overhaul and restructure it. Just because conversion does not prosper under current circumstances does not mean that it does not work under other conditions. We Jews have shown remarkable capability to achieve in many realms of human endeavor. It is difficult to believe that the Jewish community would actually fail if it made a serious effort at proactive conversion.

Beyond Our Means

The sixth argument against proactive conversion is that the Jewish community cannot afford to do it. Lack of resources is an argument used constantly in government and the voluntary sector to indicate that the expenditure in question has lower priority than other programs, projects, or institutions. There is little that the Jewish community has chosen to do that it has not been able to afford. Institutions such as synagogues often say that they cannot afford an innovative program of one kind or another; yet when the roof begins to leak and an "emergency fund" is needed, the money is somehow found. In truth, the Jewish community can afford what it wants to afford. The resources within the community are vast enough to undertake multiple efforts.

The Arguments Against Conversion in Sum

Mixing all of these anticonversion arguments together does indeed create a series of high and seemingly insurmountable hurdles. Let us distill them into one argument we are likely to hear in so many words.

There is no tradition in Judaism for open conversion (opponents say), and with good reason: *Halacha* forbids it. We should take care of our own first. If this venture goes too far, the antisemites will come after us. Even if the antisemites remain dormant and we ignore the *Halachic* restrictions, these programs will never work.

Besides, it costs a fortune to implement programs that will never work. That is the end of that. Period.

Focusing on Israel as a Diversion

It is no accident that conversion is the issue over which American Jews have drawn the battle lines between ourselves and the religious "extremists" in Israel. American Jews are insecure enough about accepting the permeable walls within our culture and our families; we are struggling on our own about legitimizing who is really Jewish and who is not. We are attempting to overcome our own fears of internal dissolution.

The religious right in Israel make us feel worse and self-righteous at the same time. It threatens American Jews in two fundamental ways. The Jewish fear of the future necessitates that Israel be a safe haven from persecution in the United States. No questions. But the who-is-a-Jew debate threatens that certainty. At the same time, we have to come to some understanding and comfort level about our own assimilation. The Israeli ultra-Orthodox make us afraid that we are going to disappear from lack of true identity. The who-is-a-Jew debates on religious pluralism bring out our fears of antisemitism *and* dissolution at the same time. The results are powerfully negative.

The fears surrounding intermarriage, loss, and tribal extinction therefore overflow into the relationship between American Jews and Israel. It is somehow odd, yet no surprise, that American Jews are locking horns with Israel as they have never done before: over the issue of conversion. It is perhaps the most convoluted of battles.

Multiple aspects of American Jewish thoughts and emotions are at play in American opposition to a law being considered by the Knesset to recognize only conversions done by Orthodox rabbis in Israel as legitimate. This has always been the de facto case. American Jews are angry, bitter, and positional enough about the issue for

Reform and Conservative denominational leaders to call for American Jews to stop giving money to the United Jewish Appeal or other organizations that support the "government" of Israel (although the UJA does not give money to the Israeli government). It is inconceivable that such calls could be made over any other issue.

The conflict is variously called the religious-pluralism crisis, the who-is-a-Jew crisis, or the conversion crisis. The same thread weaves through them. First, American Jews are appalled by the notion of a theocracy, the breakdown of walls between church and state—in America, Iran, or Israel. It is separation of government from religion that protects Jews in America. Throughout history, the fusion of state and religion have meant only disaster for Jews. The vast majority of Jews do not want nonelected religious leaders in Israel formulating governmental policy. More frightening is the specter of elected religious leaders making policy that delegitimizes other religious groups. Because the gulf between ultra-Orthodox Jews and other Jews is so wide and widening, American Jews cannot tolerate the notion of ultra-Orthodox Jews controlling Israel.

Israel was meant to be a homeland to all Jews, a haven from repression and disenfranchisement of any kind. The great majority of Jews are horrified that they might be delegitimized or made second-class citizens again—by other Jews!

American Jews love Israel. It makes them feel proud and safe; it gives them a sense of self unlike anything in modern times. They feel that Israel belongs to all Jews. American Jews may have issues with particular government policies, on the wars Israel has fought and on the peace process and the relationship to Palestinians. The emotional ties to Israel that would emerge in a heartbeat if Israel were threatened by an outside enemy, and if Jewish lives were in danger, is unthreatened by any issue, except one. Pluralism. Who is a Jew. Conversion.

The ascendance of right-wing orthodoxy into the political life of Israel clearly threatens the American identity of American Jews vis-à-vis the church-state issue. But it also threatens their Jewish identity. Most American Jews (85 percent) are not Orthodox. Of those who are, many are modern Orthodox, that is, they are traditional Jews in terms of ritual practice but are largely integrated into the fabric of American society. The vast majority are Reform, Conservative, and cultural Jews. By adopting the law of conversion, the Israeli government would give government approval to the ideology that Conservative, Reform, and Reconstructionist rabbis are not *real* rabbis, that their synagogues are not *real* synagogues and they are not *real* Jews.

Most American Jews are not moving to Israel. But that does not matter. What if they wanted to? Needed to? Thousands of non-Jews related to Jews from the former Soviet Union populate Israel and continue to come as part of the great *aliyah* from Russia and Central Asia. Will they be allowed fifty years from now if the ultra-Orthodox are firmly in control? These are not scenarios American Jews want to consider. Israel's openness to them and its connections to all Jews cannot be compromised. So Jewish groups in America are willing to go to extreme measures, taking issue with Israel as never before.

Israel serves as a mirror to the intensity of emotion felt by American Jews over these issues and their inability to face them at home. The battle, after all, is over a *conversion* law *in Israel*. It says nothing about conversions by rabbis outside of Israel. Is it so threatening because American Jews love Israel so much and cannot stand this symbol drifting away from them? Yes. And more.

The who-is-a-Jew rhetoric asks a nonrhetorical question about what makes a Jew, what it means to be a Jew, how participation in Jewish peoplehood is defined. Who has the right to say who is in and who is out, and what are the criteria? What is meaningful participation, and what is marginal? What are the rules for admission and the behavioral standards for identification as a Jew?

All of these questions are raised, and the focus is entirely on Israel. American Jews are determined to keep the ultra-Orthodox from telling us who we are not. But we do not begin to really tackle the issue at home. We could ask all the same questions about conversion in the United States. Yet the topic is hardly on the radar screen of the American Jewish community. We would much rather focus our emotional and intellectual energy on conversion issues in Israel than at home. It is almost as if we have no conversion issues at home. That most non-Jewish spouses do not convert seems to be lost in the hoopla about Israel's conversion stance and our own prevention strategies. Somehow or the other, we scream and yell and fight and lobby about conversion in Israel, and the connections of the topic in America are lost. If issues about conversion matter in Israel, then they must matter here. We cannot seem to make the obvious bridge.

But here it is. Considering issues of religious pluralism, defining standards for conversion, and thinking about how one behaves as a Jew are vital issues—for Israel and for America. We cannot deflect thinking about it at home simply because it is too difficult, too painful, too uncertain. Battle cries about the who-is-a-Jew issue in Israel and prevention of intermarriage in America reflect the same fear about the survival and meaning of Judaism. These battles, however, cannot substitute for the positive processes of defining who we are and what we want to be, and how the definitions and standards involve both born Jews and the millions who are already part of our families or might become part of them.

The who-is-a-Jew issue strikes a raw nerve because so many of our families already include non-Jews. What if they wanted to be Jews? How would that work? In the meantime, are the ultra-Orthodox suggesting that if I, the father or mother, grandfather or grandmother, am lucky enough to have a non-Jewish member of my family become a Jew, this is not good enough? The last thing any Jew wants to hear is that there is no winning, that a Reform or Conservative conversion is not good enough. This seems both insulting and hopeless to most American Jews.

The battle can take some ugly turns. Although the issue is supposed to pertain only to conversion in Israel, there is already spillover. As the *Forward* reports:

Under the Law of Return, all Jews are allowed to immigrate to Israel. Earlier this week, the Yisrael family, which converted to Judaism in 1988 through a Conservative rabbinic court at California, was detained at Ben-Gurion airport instead of being welcomed as new immigrants. . . . "The Interior Ministry has no right to refuse our converts from outside of Israel. They nonetheless have been doing so. This is especially so when they are of color," the director of the (Conservative) Rabbinical Assembly of Israel, Rabbi Andrew Sacks, wrote in an e-mail obtained by the *Forward*. "I have been trying to sound the wake up call. Now such converts are being held in custody. Outrageous but true," Rabbi Sacks wrote [Gootman, 1998, p. 1].

The intensity of the issue allows us to direct our attention elsewhere. We do not have to really address conversion issues in the United States so long as Israel allows us an outlet for such powerful emotions. It is a convenient and powerful side-tracking barrier.

What Do We (Really) Think About Converts?

Almost every Jew is likely to say that converts make good Jews. Most of us probably think that we completely welcome converts. We say that converts are fully equal in our synagogues. We say that no one would discourage a potential convert from embracing Judaism and that rabbis encourage individuals to study and become part of the Jewish people. Most of us would be shocked to learn that the welcome mat is not really out as much as we think it is and that potential converts and those who have successfully navigated the process sometimes feel like second-class citizens—or even inauthentic Jews.

How often born Jews, in casual conversation, say, "You know, she's a convert," or "He converted." Someone may say "She's a convert" ten or twenty or forty years after the fact. What does this suggest? It is often said with admiration: "She's a better Jew than I am." But there is still an element of surprise or uncertainty hidden in the delineation: a not-born Jew always came from someplace else, and his or her Jewish credentials are therefore somehow never quite the same as for a born Jew. Most of us cannot hear how our words sound to converts or potential converts because we do not intend to be hurtful, but our language and mind-set may transmit harsh connotations.

The sincerity of potential converts should not be as serious a question as it was eight hundred years ago or even one hundred years ago. People might choose to be a Jew for good reasons. Being a Jew may be seen as desirable and positive. Judaism can offer a great deal of spiritual and community support to any individual who chooses to belong. Why should Jews be suspicious of the sincerity of those who are already deeply religious but are looking for the right faith tradition in which to express it? Why should we be suspicious of people longing for community and seeing Jewish peoplehood as offering comfort in the context of America?

For those who claim that initial rejection, rigid selectiveness, testing, and keeping the gates closed are part of the standards that are embedded in *Halacha*—for those who interpret the words of the Torah to sustain them—there is little or nothing to say other than there are other rabbinic and scholarly interpretations. One cannot argue with God's truth except with some other interpretation of God's truth. Fortunately, Judaism is filled with the rich tradition of multiple, diverse, and ever-changing interpretations of what constitutes God's truth. Some laws or traditions do (and ought to) become relegated to the Jewish past.

But we Jews cannot say out of the other side of our mouths that the preferred entrance to our world is through bloodline. As a community, we posit an implicit inequality in the merit of the marriage and in the quality of the family by saying, "We didn't want you as our first choice, but now we welcome you with open arms." Judaism must open up its psychological and institutional gates for real. Some standards should be maintained for ritual conversion. But suspicion, testing, second-guessing, and reluctance are tremendous emotional and practical barriers.

Does anyone really believe that the non-Jew, a potential convert, does not hear "First choice is to marry a born Jew—but then, and only then, if that does not work out, a convert is better than a mixed marriage, which amounts to an illness, a war, and a holocaust"? In effect, "A convert is one step better than disease and disaster"? Protestation that this is not the message, that converts are fully part of the Jewish people, that the Jewish community welcomes them and considers them the same as a born Jew is denial.

There is an emotional no-win in how many Jews view converts. On the one hand, we are unlike them because they are not Jewish; that is, they are strangers. On the other hand, if converts become Jews through the religious door, then the born Jew is unlike them because they themselves are not religious Jews. Coupled with the notion that Judaism or being Jewish is a feeling that one absorbs through growing up—grandparent memories and so on—then someone who does not grow up Jewish cannot be like me because they have not had these experiences. Since Judaism is a culture, not a religion, and since culture is a product of childhood and experience, then no one can *become* a Jew.

Individuals may erect their own barriers to converts. Perhaps we ourselves do not want to be "religious" Jews. Many Jews have their own familial and religious baggage—bad experience with a parent, a negative interaction with a rabbi, an unsatisfactory experience in Hebrew school. Many Jews have anti-Jewish baggage of their own, and non-Jewish spouses who want to explore Jewish life may bring all or some of these experiences to the forefront. The gates closed to converts, therefore, are not only ideological and institutional but also very personal. Ignorance, embarrassment, hostility, shame, and a whole range of emotions may keep individuals from welcoming converts or encouraging them to Judaism.

The conversion survey in Exhibit 4.1 should be a required reality check for all Jews. We need to go beneath the surface to know how we really think and feel about ourselves and potential converts. Do we believe that someone is Jewish because he or she has Jewish blood or Jewish genes? How would we feel if a majority of individuals in our synagogue were converts? Would we rather that our child or grandchild married somebody who was born Jewish with two Jewish parents rather than someone who has one Jewish parent? Do we still refer to somebody as a convert if he or she has been Jewish for a long time? Would we feel comfortable if a majority of Jews in America were Black, Asian, and Latino? These and many other questions posed in Exhibit 4.1 can be used to assess our own feelings about race, ethnicity, and our true openness to outsiders. Our conceptions of Judaism may be constrained by images of people who are primarily White and of Eastern European or Central European origins, sharing our predilections of language, customs, foods, and so on.

No Jew will admit to being a racist. But in their heart of hearts, some Jews believe in the idea of Jewish blood, Jewish genes, the indistinguishable and unknowable essence of Judaism, as somehow biologically determined. The strength of Judaism, of course, rests in its theology, ritual, communal structure, norms, values, common history, language, and culture. These are learned and absorbed. They are transmitted by deed, action, education, experience, and participation, not by genetic code. To believe otherwise is to believe, at some base level, that no convert, no matter how passionate or how much he or she believes in and practices Judaism, can be a *real* Jew.

Judaism is not a race. Rabbi Daniel Gordis (1997), vice president of the University of Judaism, argues that there is no inherent biological "chosenness" in being Jewish. If there were, how would we account for the long history of Jewish conversion? Rather, Jewish birthright comes from living a Jewish life, a choice that everyone, born Jewish or non-Jewish, can make. If there is no such reality as Jewish genes, Jewish blood, or Jewish biology, then the gates must be open to any and all who choose to be part of the Jewish people. Those who are born Jews receive the gift of participation at birth.

Exhibit 4.1. Conversion Survey

Do you strongly agree, agree, disagree, or strongly disagree with the following statements?

Statement	Strongly agree	Agree	Disagree	Strongly disagree
1. A large number of converts would add to Judaism by bringing in fresh ideas, new blood, and new content.	☐	☐	☐	☐
2. I might feel uncomfortable if a majority of Jews were converts as opposed to born Jews.	☐	☐	☐	☐
3. I would like my child or grandchild to marry someone who was born Jewish with two Jewish parents, rather than someone who has only one Jewish parent.	☐	☐	☐	☐
4. A convert is as much a Jew as a born Jew.	☐	☐	☐	☐
5. I would like to see the number of Jews doubled or tripled in the United States through non-Jews choosing to convert to Judaism.	☐	☐	☐	☐
6. I believe a convert must study Judaism for a year before becoming Jewish.	☐	☐	☐	☐
7. Being Jewish is something biological.	☐	☐	☐	☐
8. I might feel uncomfortable if a majority of Jews were Black, Asian, or Latino.	☐	☐	☐	☐
9. Converts can never be as Jewish as someone born and raised as a Jew because they did not grow up with Jewish grandparents, Jewish foods, and a general Jewish feeling.	☐	☐	☐	☐

Do you strongly agree, agree, disagree, or strongly disagree with the following statements?

	Strongly agree	Agree	Disagree	Strongly disagree
10. It should be easy to convert to Judaism, with simple and clear rules.	☐	☐	☐	☐
11. I believe that there is something called a Jewish soul.	☐	☐	☐	☐
12. I would like my child or grandchild to marry someone who was born Jewish rather than someone who converted to Judaism.	☐	☐	☐	☐
13. I believe that the Jewish community is very open to any non-Jew who would like to convert to Judaism.	☐	☐	☐	☐
14. Jews are a race.	☐	☐	☐	☐
15. Too many converts could have a negative effect on the Jewish people.	☐	☐	☐	☐
16. Someone is Jewish because he or she has Jewish blood or Jewish genes.	☐	☐	☐	☐
17. I would like to see more converts who are Black, Asian, or Latino.	☐	☐	☐	☐
18. A convert often makes a better Jew than a born Jew does.	☐	☐	☐	☐
19. Someone who is considering becoming a Jew should be carefully screened to make sure his or her motives are sincere.	☐	☐	☐	☐
20. I might feel uncomfortable if the majority of individuals in my synagogue were converts.	☐	☐	☐	☐
21. Marrying someone who is Jewish is a good reason to choose to convert to Judaism.	☐	☐	☐	☐
22. I still refer to someone who has converted to Judaism as a convert, even if he or she has been Jewish for a long time.	☐	☐	☐	☐

We choose to call someone who is born of a Jewish mother a Jew. The religious norms of the group have defined participation primarily through the bloodline of the mother. The Reform movement has challenged the norm and been accused of splitting the Jewish people. These self-imposed guidelines should be reevaluated constantly. Some even-newer construct may be appropriate.

Jews do not have biological makeup different from that of other human beings. Other racial groups deal with the same issues. Does a drop of Black blood make someone Black? How does someone who is a quarter, an eighth, or a sixteenth of some particular racial or ethnic group identify himself or herself? When is the blood pure and when is it impure? Of course, Jews would be appalled by these questions if asked by Nazis or others seeking to do Jews harm. It would be terrible if we imposed racist definitions of Judaism upon ourselves.

The questions we need to ask ourselves should be part of Jewish organizational seminars, workshops, retreats, and family discussions. We need to check our own pulse on the questions of Exhibit 4.1:

Do you agree?

Disagree?

Do you feel that Jews are a race?

Do you believe that your synagogue is open?

How do you know?

How do you evaluate?

How do you judge?

Think about this set of premises—truths or untruths—and see where you fall; where your family, friends, and acquaintances do; and the organizations and institutions to which you belong. Are these questions that you ever think about or discuss? They should be.

Notes

1. For a more detailed view of this argument, see these readings in Epstein (1995): B. Z. Wachholder, "Attitudes Towards Proselytizing in the Classical Halakah" (pp. 15–32); M. Goodman, "Proselytizing in Rabbinic Judaism" (pp. 33–45); and J.H.A. Wijnhoven, "The Zohar and the Proselyte" (pp. 47–65).

5

Walls We Have Built
Against Potential Converts

The Jewish organizational and institutional network in America holds an essential key to unlocking the gates. The first contact that an interested non-Jew has with the "official" Jewish community can determine if that person decides to proceed with or withdraw from the process of becoming a Jew. Potential members of our community—those we would want and cherish—may be left standing before the institutional gates, wondering what magic words will open them; or when the gates have already opened a crack, wondering what to do next if no one is standing behind them. If we are to consider the vital role that proactive conversion might play in building the Jewish community of the future, we must next examine where conversion fits in today's institutional landscape and identify existing obstacles to proactive conversion.

The Jewish institutional world is neither monolithic nor stagnant, nor is there a singular approach to any one issue. The various organizations and institutions within the community range in focus from the very broad to the very narrow, from the multifaceted and wide-reaching United Jewish Appeal, for example, to the laserlike focus of small Jewish human service agencies across America.

Issues within the community can be categorized in three sets. The broadest concerns are *civil issues*, which encompass both domestic and international questions: antisemitism, Israel and Middle East policy, the former Soviet Union, Holocaust education and remembrance. The second set are *human service issues*: senior housing, family services, Jewish community centers, and so on. The third important area of concern within the landscape is *religious*. We devote a great deal of our philanthropic dollars and "Jewish" time to synagogues and other religious institutions.

A subset of the religious world is *identity formation*: Jewish day schools, summer camps, after-school youth programs, adult education, and other efforts to keep us connected and identified as Jews. Further down the ladder of Jewish identity is the issue of *intermarriage*, which has received increasing attention and time (although little financial investment) since the 1990 National Jewish Population Study (NJPS) was released in 1992. Finally, last in order of importance is the issue of *conversion*. Relative to other concerns capturing attention (and time, money, and passion) on the vast Jewish institutional landscape, conversion is a solitary tree standing far off on the horizon. Little wonder, with so many other less threatening issues.

This is not to say that no one in the institutional structure is concerned about conversion. Some of our important thinkers and community leaders are beginning to write and speak passionately about this issue to an increasingly interested audience; Chapter Eight examines what they are saying and doing. Apart from these few exemplars, other players in the institutional world deal with conversion only as a matter of necessity, and then rarely and often not very well. This chapter looks at those institutions; at what they think, say, and do; and at how their thoughts, words, and deeds affect those who come knocking at the gates.

A Flyover of the Landscape

Much like Jewish identity in America, the Jewish institutional landscape divides itself along religious and civil lines. The preponderance of institutions affiliated or concerned with Jewish life fall into the civil/human services realm, where conversion has little or no place.

A brief flyover of the landscape reveals in which corner of the vast Jewish institutional terrain the issue of conversion resides. Even this geographical approach is revealing: for the most part, when we look at a map of the Jewish world, conversion appears to be a regional (read: religious) concern, and one that, on the current map, seems unlikely to take on "national" significance without a dedicated effort to change how we approach these borders. (Even under exclusively Jewish auspices, information about conversion is limited. The sixty-three-page *Judaica Book Guide* for fall 1998, for example, contains only two books about conversion.)

The Civil Division

At the center of the Jewish civil world lie the enormous and highly visible fundraising organizations that distribute money, domestically and internationally. (The exception to the civil focus of these fundraising organizations has been around the issue of religious pluralism—and thereby, conversion—in Israel, as discussed in Chapter Four.) The largest of these institutions is the network of United Jewish Appeal and local federations.

The federation system supports the human service side of civil Jewish life, from Jewish homes for the aged to Jewish summer camps, from Jewish vocational services and bureaus of Jewish education to Jewish family and children's services and Jewish community centers. Some of these institutions are almost entirely dependent on their local federation (the local "Jewish United Way") for funds; for others, the federation provides only a small portion of the budget. Each year, the federation campaigns raise about $750 million, a portion of which goes for use in Israel and elsewhere overseas. Formal institutional involvement from the federation world to deal with intermarriage and conversion issues is rare; federations generally focus specifically on continuity and Jewish education to deal with the issue of intermarriage.

Other Institutions

In addition to these human service and fundraising structures, the Jewish community landscape encompasses a range of self-funded institutions that deal with other aspects of Jewish civil life. Many of these are membership organizations: B'nai Brith, Hadassah, the National Council of Jewish Women, Jewish War Veterans, and so on. These groups, although Jewish in their membership and focus, raise money for hospitals, for example, or engage in other community-oriented activities. There are also Jewish political organizations across the political spectrum that concern themselves with defense against antisemitism and legislation affecting the Jewish community and Israel. In addition, at both the national and local levels are educational, service delivery, and other cultural groups and organizations. Finally, a growing number of Jewish foundations, which exist outside the constraints and politics of the formal fundraising structures, are becoming increasingly important players in the Jewish institutional landscape.

The Religious Division

Many American Jews identify themselves as cultural or secular, as opposed to religious, Jews. They may give to Jewish charities, support Jewish causes, and believe that it is important to ensure the future of the Jewish people. For many, including cultural Jews, the future includes sustaining the religious aspects of Judaism, even if they themselves do not practice the religion. Yet most of the Jewish institutional landscape remains primarily cultural and largely separate from the religious institutions of Judaism. The desire for these divisions has diminished, but the chasm is still difficult to bridge.

Similarly, just as the civil government of the United States does not provide financial support for religious institutions, the civil structures of the Jewish community do not provide much funding for the religious ones. Jewish religious institutions, especially synagogues, are almost entirely self-sustaining, relying on membership dues,

High Holiday ticket sales, and other nonfederation funding sources. Some federations are beginning to support synagogues, but the investment is relatively small.

The religious landscape also has its own organizational structure, drawn along denominational lines, both nationally and locally. At the national level, each denomination has at least one seminary to train its rabbis and a synagogue organization that provides some support services to congregations, as well as a forum from which to determine denominational guidelines and policy. The rabbis from the denominations also have their own national organizations, each of which sets guidelines and procedures for its member rabbis.

Despite the apparent centralization of the denominational structure, this world is by no means unified, or even highly aligned in terms of ideology or action. This is an important principle in the discussion of conversion: although the various seminaries, denominations, and rabbinic associations may publish guidelines and policies, individual synagogues and individual rabbis implement and interpret the guidelines. Since most of the Jewish institutional structure treats conversion as a purely religious issue (whatever its implications for the rest of the Jewish world), the individual synagogues and rabbis become the most important institutional players in determining the reception as a potential convert approaches the gates. More than any policy or guideline, a negative or even neutral response from the representatives of the synagogue—administrative staff, synagogue executives, members of the congregation, and others—can be a daunting structural barrier to a potential convert. (This chapter examines all relevant aspects of the Jewish institutional world except rabbis; Chapter Six examines the role of the individual rabbi in this context.)

Synagogues are democratic entities with a wide variance in opinion and culture. There are often tensions within the lay structure, between the professional and lay leaders. Rabbis and congregants are frequently at odds concerning issues of mixed marriage. The boards of synagogues tend to be very cautious, especially since they are so concerned with maintaining the viability of an institution that is often beset by financial, membership, and logistical woes of all kinds. Synagogues may undertake programmatic initiatives; they rarely engage in initiatives that take them too far away, or move them too fast, from their central mission or their way of operating. Innovative programs of one type or another bubble up from the congregations; these tend to be more isolated than systemic. They tend not to be replicated very much, and their life span is often limited.

Systemic change within the synagogue community is possible and widespread initiatives in this realm are conceivable, but usually they are jump-started from the outside. It is not likely that major new initiatives in the realm of conversion will develop within the synagogue structure. Once programs have been demonstrated to work and can be shown to benefit the synagogue community, then there may be a snowball effect and a greater number of synagogues could jump in to participate.

Finally, there is one last institution that does not usually appear on the map of the Jewish institutional landscape but that directly affects how we think, feel, and behave as Jews in America. The *family*, which includes both the Jewish partner and Jewish in-laws in the case of intermarriage, and the non-Jewish family in all cases, can throw up surprising and powerful obstacles when a non-Jew begins the process of becoming a Jew, or be great facilitators.

Expanding Conversion on the Map

The Jewish institutional structure treats conversion as a religious issue, one that belongs to the synagogues, seminaries, and rabbis. This is apparent both in the absence of programs, funds, and initiatives coming from the civil side of the landscape and from the fierce protectiveness the religious side demonstrates concerning the issue. Civil institutions do not attempt to interpret Jewish law, under which the religious guidelines for conversion clearly fall. Nonetheless, it is significant that the civil institutions, which consistently argue and debate the issue of Jewish continuity and the survival of the Jewish people, are not currently looking at conversion as part of the solution.

If we are to build a Jewish community of the future that includes welcoming non–born Jews into the *community* and not just into the *synagogue*, this segregation of issues must change. Standards for conversion, of course, should remain in the hands of the religious institutions, but standards are the means by which someone *officially* becomes a Jew. Becoming part of the Jewish people means becoming a fully integrated Jewish citizen welcome across the entire community, not just in the religious portion of the map. The entire community must begin to rethink how we can accomplish this goal.

We are a long way from moving conversion onto the civil Jewish agenda. The final chapter of this book explores our means of expanding the presence and importance of conversion in the Jewish community; this chapter looks at where we are today. Considering the currently segregated institutional landscape, this chapter can focus solely on Jewish religious institutions and the family. At the moment, these are the only Jewish institutions taking any action—welcoming or unwelcoming—regarding conversion.

The Walls

When a non-Jew begins the process of exploring Judaism, the individual may encounter walls at any stage of the process, walls that appear either scalable or insurmountable. Walls are not equivalent to standards. Standards ensure that becoming a Jew is a rigorous, serious, and heartfelt process; walls are barriers that we erect from fear, ignorance, a sense of superiority or inferiority, or perhaps just plain laziness.

The institutional walls a non-Jew interested in Judaism may encounter at any point along the path fall into three main categories: *policy*, *structure*, and *procedure*. The following sections examine these barriers in depth.

Policy Barriers

Policy walls are those impersonal barriers that derive from the resolutions, guidelines, edicts, and curricula of the denominational structures or individual synagogue administrations. Policy is reflective of ideology; which in turn drives priorities and programs. Organizations and institutions have both formal and informal policies. What is written is not always what is implemented, but the ideological doctrinal statements—the guidelines for practices and the formal edicts expressed through constitutional bylaws or resolutions of assemblies—demonstrate what organizations and institutions are likely to do concerning conversion.

The policies may be directly related to conversion (the rabbinic guidelines on the conversion process), or they may be indirectly related (the policy describing who may be a member of the synagogue, who may sit on the synagogue board, who may become a *bar* or *bat mitzvah*, and so on). Indirect policies are often more insidious barriers to proactive conversion because they can, under the guise of advancing or protecting the interests of those who are already inside, stand in the way of a potential convert's progress on the path toward becoming a Jew.

Official denominational policies ultimately are filtered through what happens in real life in ordinary communities and synagogues. Constant redefinition, interpretation, and change are the order of the day. National policy may set tones, and tone may facilitate or inhibit new initiatives from taking form on a national level. Usually, however, changes bubble up from the bottom, and denominational policies reflect what is already happening, giving legitimacy to what is rather than creating change. Policies that do not reflect the "real world" tend to be ignored. The thousands and millions of individuals (lay and professional), institutions, and programs that weave the fabric of the community change national policy. On the other hand, norms redefined at the top can help move along people who might be stuck, wanting to change and needing the legitimacy of the movements to help them along.

Standard Bearers—or Barriers?

Each denomination has standards—guidelines—for the actual process of conversion. Not surprisingly, these standards are consistent with the strictness or flexibility of the denomination's adherence to *Halacha*. The Orthodox movement's standards are the most strict, the Conservative's somewhat less so, and so on. Even though standards are not the equivalent of walls, they may function as barriers to a potential convert who does not understand them and cannot readily find help in interpreting what to do.

For example, the rabbis of the Orthodox movement, represented by the Commission on *Gerut* (conversion) of the Rabbinical Council of America (RCA), sponsor and perform conversions according to their close reading of *Halacha*. It is certainly possible for an interested non-Jew to become a Jew through an Orthodox conversion.[1] Still, one cannot easily wander in through the Orthodox gates. Navigating this system requires knowledge obtained through potential marriage to a Jew or through a willful attempt to keep pushing. According to Rabbi Stephen Dworken, executive vice president of the RCA, there is no written information available on conversion programs sponsored by the Rabbinical Council. Instead, Orthodox conversion is "based on a course of study with a sponsoring rabbi who can deal with [proselytes] in their intellectual quest and their spiritual quest, all, of course, within a *Halachic* framework."

Another Orthodox rabbi, Myron Zuber, explained in response to a request for written information on Orthodox conversions that everything was in Hebrew. He believed for the serious potential convert, however, there was plenty to read. Indeed, the only written conversion guidelines available for this book from the official Orthodox movement were in very small type—and in Hebrew. (Orthodox guidelines do appear, in English, in several secondary resources.)

That is not to say that the Orthodox movement does not have positive practices and policies. Certain Orthodox approaches are often quite appealing to potential converts. The rigor and certainty, the toughness of having to push through, may appeal to some individuals who wish to become Jews.

Some standards are meant to be barriers; they are intended to weed out the "insincere." Traditionally, when a potential convert approaches a rabbi, the rabbi is supposed to turn that person away three times. In both the Conservative and Reform movements, this tradition has been transformed into an in-depth interview with the interested non-Jew. The Committee on Jewish Law and Standards of the Rabbinical Assembly (Conservative) instructs rabbis not to agree immediately to begin the process of conversion. Instead, the rabbi should probe interested non-Jews about their family background, their religious commitment, and their motivation for seeking a place in the Jewish community.[2]

The Committee on Conversion of the Central Conference of American Rabbis (Reform) also suggests that their rabbis test the proselyte "to understand the religious and personal background of the prospective convert, and to discuss his/her motivation for wishing to explore conversion" (Central Conference of American Rabbis Committee on Conversion, 1998).

Is this test necessary? Most people make the decision to begin the process of conversion after much thought, soul-searching, and anguish, or the inquiry itself may lead to a more intense searching process. Finding Judaism is a relief, a joyous event. For example, at the beginning of her journey toward Judaism, Margaret found that the first time she "came to the Temple, I felt as if I had finally found a part of myself that had been lost for a long time. A oneness, a quiet peace of mind that my values and ideals were not out of place in the world." What further tests of sincerity are needed? How many dedicated and passionate potential Jews such as this woman have we turned away by testing them through what some may consider an offensive interview?

Andrea, married to a born Jew, decided to convert after living in Israel, where she felt "like a Jewish soul returning home" (Conversion to Judaism home page, Oct. 11, 1997). She and her husband initially "approached a Conservative rabbi, who discouraged us from every angle. Not knowing that this was what rabbis were supposed to do, we literally went 'shopping' for a rabbi." Others may not be so persistent.

When he was a Methodist child in a small town, Paul discovered the *Sh'ma* (the most common Jewish prayer, the principle statement of Jewish faith and belief) and began to recite it several times a day. As an adult, when he made his "first step toward conversion and met with an Orthodox rabbi, [he] was turned away" without explanation and never told that he had to try two more times. He, too, began a search for a rabbi, until he found one who would welcome him into the community he had longed to join since he was a child.

Barriers of Context

Another wall to proactive conversion is the context in which the national synagogue associations create policy for "welcoming" non-Jews into the Jewish community. Although the rabbinic associations for each movement establish conversion guidelines for its member rabbis to follow, the synagogue associations deal with conversion reluctantly.

As discussed in Chapter Three, the trend in most of the Jewish community as regards dealing with intermarriage is toward prevention; conversion, when it appears in the policy statements, is a secondary concern. The synagogue associations have yet to convene a commission or issue a resolution addressing proactive conversion outside of the intermarriage debate. This is true across denominations, although policy splits along denominational lines. The Orthodox and Conservative movements generally take a more hard-line approach. The Reform and Reconstructionist movements remain more open to new ideas, but even Reform, which remains at the forefront of outreach efforts, is beginning to incorporate prevention. (Outside of the denominational structure, a few institutions and organizations have evolved that deal directly with issues of conversion, but they are rare on the landscape, fledglings without major impact in the vast Jewish organizational and institutional network. Chapter Eight examines these programs.)

Semibarriers

We do not know exactly what to do about those non-Jews who want to become a part of us, especially those who come to Judaism through marriage. We feel so much conflict about their presence among us that we erect semibarriers: policies that simultaneously make them feel welcome and keep them at a distance.

For example, the Leadership Council of Conservative Judaism issued in March 1995 a "statement on intermarriage" that outlines the Conservative movement's unified stance on intermarriage and conversion. (The Leadership Council is a joint effort of the several national Conservative organizations: the Federation of Jewish Men's Clubs, the Jewish Theological Seminary of America, the Rabbinical Assembly, the United Synagogue of Conservative Judaism, and the Women's League for Conservative Judaism.) The statement describes a policy for educating and converting those who are reluctantly being admitted to the community: "If, despite efforts at prevention, an intermarriage seems likely to occur, we must encourage halakhic conversion to Judaism." As the statement explains: "We should make this process as inviting as possible so that the potential convert feels warmly accepted by our community in the hopes of helping that person embrace our people and our traditions with the utmost of sincerity. We know that sincere Jews-by-choice add enthusiasm and strength to our community. They enrich us by their adult understanding of Jewish values, by their quest for spiritual sustenance, and by their commitment to a Jewish way of life."

Yet the very same document concludes with a lengthy reaffirmation of the standards concerning intermarriage and conversion as set forth by the Committee on Jewish Law and Standards of the Rabbinical Assembly. Among the standards are those limiting the participation of non-Jews in synagogue life: "Only Jews may be members of Conservative congregations and affiliated organizations. However, non-Jewish partners are welcome to attend services and to participate in educational and social programs."

Which way is the right way? How far into the synagogue is the non-Jew allowed to step before the walls come up?

Barriers in Limiting the Welcome

The Reform movement, which began formal outreach in 1983 in part to "welcome and provide education and support for those who seek to investigate Judaism" (Commission on Reform Jewish Outreach, 1997), still has not resolved its conflicted position on non-Jews in the synagogue. Outreach seeks to make them feel welcome, but other resolutions and initiatives of the Union of American Hebrew Congregations (UAHC) place limits on how welcome they actually are. In a separate move, the UAHC, in its statement on "Enrollment Policies in Reform Religious Schools," resolved to "encourage congregations to . . . establish a clearly articulated policy that offers enrollment in Reform religious schools and day schools only to children who are not receiving formal religious education in any other religion" (Commission on Reform Jewish Outreach, n.d. [a]). On the surface, this resolution makes sense: we do not want Christian children (or children of any other religion) to bring their ideas into our schools, and we want to encourage parents to bring up their children in one religious faith. On the other hand, the resolution implies that we should extend only so far the hand of outreach to children of interfaith marriages. They may be among us, as long as they are wholly of us. If they are still struggling, good-bye.

What, then, are the real policies in the Jewish institutional world regarding the place of non-Jews? Should we take the safest route and keep them outside the gates, whatever their connections

to our families and our community? Or, as the Conservative movement declares, should "sincere Jews by choice . . . be warmly welcomed in our community"? (Leadership Council, 1995). It seems
that we, the insiders, cannot decide how we feel about those non-
Jews (our family, our friends) standing at the gate.

Structural Barriers

Whatever we may say in our policies and declarations, it is up to
the individual synagogues and rabbis to create a structure in which
to interpret and implement them. At this point, the synagogues and
rabbis become the gatekeepers to Judaism.

Synagogue Walls

The first step many potential converts take to begin the process of
exploring Judaism involves contact with a synagogue—making
inquiries on the telephone or attending services to explore. Yet that
is where walls that we want to believe do not exist pop up again
and again.

As part of the research for this book, the Institute for Jewish and
Community Research conducted a telephone survey of forty-five
synagogues across the United States. The survey presented a simple
request to the first person who answered the phone: "I am interested
in becoming Jewish, and I would like to have some information on
the process of conversion." The survey noted the respondent's tone
of voice, the outcome of the request, and information received.

For the most part, the person answering the phone at the synagogues was cold or neutral. Many of them seemed surprised or flus-
tered by the request, saying, "Well, I don't know. You'll have to talk
to the rabbi" and hurrying the caller off the phone after taking a
message. Only seven of the forty-five people who answered the
phone offered information, whether in the form of brochures on
Introduction to Judaism classes or dates and times of classes. One
person, explaining that she was not Jewish herself, conducted a
lengthy (and ultimately unsuccessful) search for a brochure that

she knew "used to be here somewhere." To be sure, some people were helpful and a few were even enthusiastic about the prospect of a potential new member of the community. The overall impression, however, was that a request for information on conversion was either surprising ("Conversion? Oh my!"), an inconvenience ("Call back when we're not so busy"), or simply unwelcome ("Ugh").

Sometimes the call reached an answering machine, and in only nine of the forty-five calls did the rabbi or someone else who might be helpful actually speak with the researcher. On the positive side, when a rabbi did speak to the caller, the rabbi's tone was warm or enthusiastic, and the information received was generally helpful.

It seems, then, that seeking information about conversion from synagogues is largely a hit-or-miss process. If the proselyte is lucky enough to catch the rabbi in the office (and American rabbis are notoriously overworked), the initial call can be a positive, welcoming experience. Before reaching the rabbi, however, the caller faces high and discouraging hurdles. It is as if some *receptionists* were trained to turn the proselyte away three times! This barrier becomes extraordinarily frustrating when the person answering the phone—a functional gatekeeper to synagogue life—throws up obstacles.

Why not give receptionists at synagogues basic information about the process of becoming a Jew? Better yet, a specific person could be trained and designated to answer inquiries about conversion. Of course, those on the synagogue telephones may treat congregants and potential congregants with equal rudeness; that is another story (but not entirely).

Most of the synagogues contacted offer or have access to an Introduction to Judaism course. How much simpler and more welcoming it would be for a potential convert to be able to gather the necessary information in a single, welcoming call rather than to have to leave a message or call back at a time when the rabbi might be available.

Inside the Shul, Outside the Community

A common suggestion to non-Jews expressing an interest in learning more about Judaism is to attend services. This idea seems a good one: participating in a Shabbat service is a pragmatic way to begin to learn about the Jewish religion, and the invitation to do so implies that the synagogue is a welcoming place, even for non-Jews. What happens inside the synagogue, however, often reinforces the suspicion on the part of potential converts and Jews-by-choice alike that unless you are born Jewish, other (born) Jews never really consider you Jewish.

The members of the congregation, who themselves may have conflicted feelings about the presence of an outsider within their walls, can pose a formidable barrier. Immediately after his conversion, Paul felt "like I was sneaked in the back door of the shul. . . . There seemed to be a bit of shame associated with being a convert. Kind of like you weren't 'really' Jewish. Being blonde and blue-eyed, I was asked frequently, 'Are you Jewish?'" Paul later left Judaism for twelve years and returned only after he found a congregation whose members did not question his right to attend.

Others feel unwelcome simply because they are not made to feel welcome. Michael, who had been "studying Judaism for several months . . . attended a synagogue once. I kind of felt like I was trespassing, so I haven't been back" (Conversion to Judaism home page, Feb. 14, 1998). We must take a hard look at what are we doing (or not doing) in our synagogues that transforms what should be a beautiful, moving, and spiritual event into one that calls for an act of bravery on the part of interested outsiders. How much Jewish spirituality is a potential convert likely to experience while hunched down in a service and hoping no one notices the intrusion?

This problem is made even worse for those who are not Caucasian. Eva found that as "an African American convert to Judaism . . . it has been very difficult for me and my converted daughter (thirteen years old) to assimilate into the Jewish community. It would be helpful to be able to connect to others like myself" (Conversion to Judaism home page, Feb. 11, 1998). It is significant that Eva is not seeking support from born Jews but from those Jews who continue to be other (the ones who might share her experiences) despite Jewish law (and policy) that commands that we treat Jews-by-choice exactly as we treat born Jews.

The boards and committees of the synagogues may prevent a convert or potential convert from feeling like a member of the community by simply never extending an invitation to join. Paul found that the brotherhood at his temple was "like a secret organization. I have never been approached about joining or receiving any information about it. I have been told it is just a bunch of 'old men' who play golf or tennis and do a social action program every once in a while." Since his conversion in 1978 and despite his many efforts to be part of the community, he still feels like he is "in a foreign culture trying to understand, build friendships and bridges and feel at home."

Getting the Word Out

We have a centuries-old tradition of not speaking too loudly about ourselves in the non-Jewish world. There have been good and practical reasons for our reticence to celebrate in public what is good and joyful about being a Jew. Now, however, we need to have the world know more about being Jewish.

Increasingly, congregations offer classes, seminars, and lecture series for those Jews and non-Jews who want to increase their knowledge of Judaism. A few congregations have begun to publicize their classes in *both* the Jewish and secular press. This trend is a positive development, and we should continue to encourage and support it.

Many of these announcements limit their audiences to those that are safe ("special opportunity for interfaith families") or place the ad only in Jewish papers. How likely is it that a non-Jew, even if curious about Judaism, is going to pick up a Jewish newspaper? Unless the announcements are in the general media, both unaffiliated Jews and nearly all non-Jews miss the information. If classes are limited to interfaith families, then thousands of people, single or married to non-Jews, are less likely to explore Judaism.

Although it is a good and positive step when congregations place announcements in the secular press inviting non-Jews to explore Judaism, the language of some ads may unwittingly negate the very intention of the ad. For example, an announcement in the secular press from a Reconstructionist synagogue in Vermont proclaims the congregation to be "progressive in style," "rich in tradition," and "open and welcoming to all." In the next line, it offers the opportunity to "study Torah, Talmud, Kabbalah, Hebrew, and more." Who is the target of this ad? A non-Jew may be interested in Judaism, yet not know what *Talmud* means, or even *Torah*. We miss the opportunity to excite and inform non-Jews about our classes, our services, and our traditions if we use language that is meaningless to them. If the congregation is "welcoming to all," why not use language that would be understood by all? We should make some attempt to explain what we mean. These pronouncements themselves could be good teaching opportunities.

"Cyberminyan"

The Internet has made vast resources available to the most remote spots on the planet—so long as there is a telephone line and a computer. Some far-thinking members of the community have started to offer information online about Judaism and conversion (see Chapter Eight). A sampling of comments from one site reveals the depth of hunger for information and support out there among prospective converts, hunger to find a community of people whose experiences are similar to their own. The writers' sense of relief at finally discovering a reliable resource about conversion is palpable. These comments, all of which were posted on the Conversion to Judaism home page, point out how little we currently do to help proselytes find what they need within the existing community structures:

"At last, a site where I can get the information I need to make the best informed decision about whether or not conversion is for me" [May 13, 1998].

"This [site] has been an answer to my 'prayers'" [May 4, 1998].

"I live in a city where there is not a great deal of support for *gerim* [converts]. I am very pleased that a site like this exists" [June 6, 1998].

"I did not know it was possible for me to become a Jew. Now visiting your page I have new hope" [July 14, 1997].

It is neither expensive nor complicated to provide a wealth of clear, up-to-date information and resources online. Remote study, even for something as personal and spiritual as conversion to Judaism, is possible via the Internet. People want to know about Judaism, and we have an obligation to tell them. Technology is making this possible; what is lacking is a unified community will to do so.

Educational Barriers

Introduction to Judaism classes can be wonderful forums to introduce non-Jews to the rich heritage of Judaism. The intention of these classes is twofold: first, to give non-Jews enough information, experience, and insight into Jewish traditions, beliefs, and customs to decide if Judaism is right for them; and second, to fulfill the study requirements for most non-Orthodox conversions. Many of those who attend these classes do not begin with the intention of converting and end up changing their minds before the class is over. These classes can be a good, positive addition to the Jewish institutional landscape—provided one can be found to suit one's schedule.

In our survey of congregations that offer Introduction to Judaism classes, the majority started classes once a year, immediately after High Holidays in the fall. All the classes in our survey were offered once a week, lasting anywhere from one-and-a-half to three hours in the evenings. Classes varied in length, some as short as twelve weeks, others as long as thirty-two, with the majority between sixteen and twenty-six weeks. In addition to the weekly class meetings, three-quarters of the courses also required that students fulfill additional requirements, from learning Hebrew to attending other supplementary courses; requirements did not differ for those who were not candidates for conversion. Cost for the class was generally low, ranging anywhere from nothing to nearly $300, with most falling into the $25–$75 range. Books generally added another $75–$150 to the cost, although several rabbis suggested that students could borrow the books from the local library.

Overall, Introduction to Judaism classes demand a solid commitment to the process of learning about Judaism. In the case of an interfaith couple, most rabbis required that both partners attend every class. For parents with children at home, three hours one evening a week is sometimes a difficult commitment to keep. Though the logic of constructing a course on Judaism to coincide with the Jewish holidays is sound, the inflexibility of starting only once a year may keep interested students away long enough for their interest to wane. Someone wanting to begin studying Judaism in November would have to wait until the following year—or go somewhere else. Finally, although the cost of the course was relatively low compared to many other adult education classes, it may be enough of a barrier to keep some prospective converts out.

Introduction to Judaism classes can be either a warm and exciting exposure to being a Jew or the last contact a non-Jew has with the Jewish institutional world. The quality of these classes varies widely, depending most often on the teaching skills and commitment of the rabbi or educator leading the course. Classes may be boring, challenging, exciting, uninspired, or simply irrelevant to the experiences of the people in the room. Students are usually a mix of Jews and non-Jews, providing a rich opportunity for cross-cultural learning.

In our survey of synagogues, most introductory courses were taught by one rabbi, with some congregations in smaller communities cooperating to offer a single course for various synagogues of the same denomination. A few other programs were multidenominational, offering perspectives on all the choices within Judaism. The structure of the classes also varied. Some were traditional lectures, with one rabbi presenting a single viewpoint for the length of the course. Others were much more creative, using a variety of books, speakers, and media to help students encounter a range of Jewish experiences. One class even included a cooking workshop to introduce students to the smells and tastes of Judaism.

Adult education is different from the supplemental schools most congregations are used to supporting, and some classes seem not to take into account the difference in how adults learn. Lan Nguyen, a reporter for *People* magazine, tracked her progress along the journey toward Judaism in "Convert's Diary," a column in the Jewish weekly newspaper *Forward*. She describes her first class: "We all sat in silence, some with eyes glazed over. The instructor had an amazing ability to lecture without pausing. We had been warned by someone at the UAHC that Wednesday's teacher could be dull, but we did not realize the energy it required to stay awake. It also didn't help that the class ran through what would have been dinner time. Subsequent nights ran along the same pattern. We sat mute in our seats, listening to the teacher talk about that night's topic" (Nguyen, 1998, p. 21).

Nguyen's experience, sadly, may be too typical of Introduction to Judaism classes. Some rabbis teach them out of obligation rather than a sense of joy. Teaching modes are often outdated. Textbooks are sometimes boring and irrelevant, both to the topics discussed in class and to the lively and dynamic world of contemporary Jewish life. Classes tend to drown students in facts and commandments, to fill them with "Jewishness." Some will drop out (and thus prove their insincerity); others will stand before the *Beit Din* at the end of their conversion process and prove their knowledge, like Ph.D. candidates defending a dissertation, often without any context for living as a Jew. It is no wonder, then, that many sincere and interested potential converts decide after their Introduction to Judaism classes not to pursue further opportunities to learn about Judaism.

Beyond the Institutional Walls

We must discard our mistrust of converts. There is something about a person who chooses—chooses!—to become a Jew that is suspect, especially to born Jews. "Why would you want to do something crazy like that?" born Jews ask of potential Jews, especially if the potential Jew is a partner or spouse. "Why make yourself the target of anti-semitism?" rabbis often inquire in their initial interviews with prose-lytes. Just to make sure this crazy person understands the gravity of this pending transformation, we create procedures—behavioral requirements—that test a convert's commitment to Judaism far beyond what would be reasonable and expected of any Jew.

If we were to implement all the right policies, disseminate clear and relevant information in all the right places, create fascinating and accessible classes across America, and systematically embrace every non-Jew who showed an interest in Judaism, we would still only be part of the way to creating a successful model of proactive conversion.

We must also mean it. That is to say, every action we take must come from a genuine desire to bring interested non-Jews into our community. If we do not mean it, then whatever the words we speak or the programs we implement, our attitude and tone betray our true feelings: we are still reluctant to let the outsider inside our gates.

Subtle Sabotage

Attitude is slippery and difficult to assess objectively. Sometimes it shows up as a casual comment or a pattern of quiet behavior. For example, prior to her own conversion, Zoe was discouraged by her Jewish mother-in-law, who told Zoe that were she not already a Jew, she would never convert. The mother-in-law, Zoe wrote, "has a lot of disagreements with Judaism, so I don't think she would care if I convert or not. But she is supportive of my conversion" (e-mail to Friends of Ruth listserv, Sept. 21, 1998). How can someone be "supportive" while denigrating Judaism and thereby the proselyte's decision to join the community? It is equivalent to tasting a plate of food, declaring it unpalatable, and then offering it to someone else on the assumption (no matter how well intended) that the second person's taste may be different. Who wants to try a dish that has been rejected by others at the table?

Acceptance and Discrimination

The most insidious and persuasive barrier to a convert's full integration into the Jewish community derives from the passionate and often heated who-is-a-Jew debate. Underlying many of the arguments swirling around in this discussion is the (secret) conviction that true membership in the Jewish community can only be achieved by birth. All other comers can never be like us, not really, not in their hearts.

But we cannot say this out loud. Instead, we let newcomers know that we know who they really are through our subtle reminders of their origins or through our nervousness at discovering that there is an outsider among us. We do not have to say anything aloud; converts sense what is in our hearts without our opening our mouths.

When she converted, Kathy found a cordial reception in the Jewish community. The rabbi and his staff "were very supportive, and the members of the Beit Din did not seem to challenge my convictions more than they needed to." She is married to a Jew, is a member of a Conservative congregation, and feels "tremendous joy in every service I attend, every holiday celebration, and every Jewish place I go." Yet this wholly Jewish woman is fearful to let other Jews know that she is a Jew by choice. "To this day I keep my conversion a secret in social situations. I never know how people will accept it, though I can't say I have been challenged, ever, about it.

I worry that some will not accept me or say I am not 'really Jewish.' I wish I could find a group or *havurah* [group or network of like-minded people] where I could be open about it."

What is shameful about having come to Judaism through means other than birth? What do we do to make it seem less legitimate to someone who finds so much joy in being Jewish? Kathy is not alone. Many Jews-by-choice find their acceptance in the Jewish community is not the joyful experience they had dreamed it would be, and there is no particular action they can point to that might justify or explain their feelings. On Web sites, in forums, in discussions around the country, converts lament the unwelcoming attitude born Jews display to them. Their decision to join the community should be a celebration for all of us.

Notes

1. Orthodox institutions do not recognize non-Orthodox conversions. This policy has created debate in the Jewish community regarding who holds the authority to define who is a Jew. Though an increasingly important topic, it is beyond the scope of this book.

2. In the three major denominations—Orthodox, Conservative, and Reform—marriage to a Jew is not a valid reason for conversion. The small Reconstructionist movement, however, does "deem marriage to a Jewish partner to be a justifiable and commendable initial reason for conversion" (Reconstructionist Rabbinical Association, 1979).

6

Rabbis at the Center of the Storm

Rabbis play an essential role in shaping communal consideration of proactive conversion. They are the most important players in facilitating or else impeding the growth of conversion to Judaism. Real life takes place between real people. Ultimately, active conversion is not only a concept but also a set of actions and interactions involving individuals, their families, and rabbis. Conversion is a composite of thoughts, conversations, communications, responses, and nonresponses. It is how people talk to each other, what they say and do not say. It is what they do and do not do. Rabbis are in the middle of many of these decisions.

In their views concerning conversion, rabbis are not very far away from the constituencies they serve and the community that they represent and sometimes lead. The wide range of emotions that they demonstrate—confusion, anger, fear, ambivalence, and so on—reflects those felt by the Jewish community as a whole. Rabbis, however, are forced to take a stand, make statements about what is right or wrong, and adjudicate this very difficult set of problems. Therefore, the rabbi becomes the focal point of the community's anxiety about acceptance or rejection and its conflicting desires to be part of the general society yet remain separate. By stating one position or the other, the rabbi can never be right. Communal ambivalence about what individuals and institutions should do to achieve mutually exclusive goals means the rabbi is always wrong, not only to groups of Jews but to individual Jews as well.

Even so, rabbis need to be much more active promoters of conversion. With their passionate belief in Judaism, they need to encourage other individuals to become part of the Jewish people. Many rabbis, however, are constrained by their own personal beliefs. Some may feel that a born Jew is better; others may believe that someone must demonstrate sincerity three times; still others may think that they should concentrate on their own congregants before expending time and energy on outsiders.

The constraints of personal thoughts and feelings among rabbis are sometimes the biggest negative influence in achieving proactive conversion. For example, Nicole had long wanted to convert to Judaism. She studied on her own, attended services, and then took the definitive step of approaching a rabbi. "I was about to convert," she said, "but at the last minute I stopped since the rabbi made it clear to me that the community would never accept me in full as Jewish" (Conversion to Judaism home page, June 12, 1997). She never again attempted to convert.

Rabbis are also buffeted by the demands of congregations, their denominational surroundings, and their own peers. The rabbinate as a whole does not encourage proactive conversion. The number of rabbis who are actually willing and able to promote conversion is limited, and the peer pressure to avoid being "too out there" on this issue is strong. As the study *Rabbis Talk About Intermarriage* (Tobin and Simon, 1999) shows, most rabbis are not emotionally or intellectually prepared to promote conversion, nor is it high on the agenda for most of them. This is not a condemnation or criticism, but a reality of current denominational thinking and where the Jewish community has been.

The rabbinate is far from homogeneous in its makeup and character, and therefore the roles of individual rabbis in the matter of conversion vary. Some rabbis are warm and personable, some are cold and off-putting. Some are people friendly, others are officious.

They may be intellectually vibrant, banal, charismatic, dull; some are engaging teachers, and others are deadly as speakers or facilitators. A potential convert can be the beneficiary or the victim of the luck of the draw. Whether or not someone chooses to initiate or complete a conversion process may largely depend on which rabbi is standing at the gate.

Hazel, for example, had remarkably bad luck: "After a quarter-century of solitary study and observance, I finally mustered the chutzpah to make some discreet inquiries. At a conservative estimate, I was rejected by some five or six rabbis of diverse denominations. (My favorite was probably the earnest, grave young Reconstructionist who met with me for one appointment. He subsequently phoned me, in a quasi-frantic manner, to cancel our second appointment and ask me never to return. He urged me to pursue imperative 'mental health counseling' for my 'severe identity crisis')" (Jewish Outreach Institute home page, July 7, 1998). She eventually did find a rabbi who was welcoming and supportive. She completed her conversion, and both she and her children became active members of a congregation.

Some rabbis are remarkably successful at encouraging conversion. They believe in promoting conversion, have the personality, and make the time. Just as there are successful institutional models, so too there are successful personal models.

Michael was lucky enough to find such a rabbi—twice. He grew up in a small town in the Pacific Northwest where there was no knowledge of Judaism, let alone actual Jews. Years later, attending a Jewish wedding, he was impressed by the rabbi and mentioned to him "a vague feeling that I had always had that I was Jewish." The rabbi suggested he begin to write about those feelings as a prelude to "examining them more closely in a formal way." Later that same year, at another Jewish wedding, he had a similar conversation with a different rabbi. "When he hears my story, how I have always felt Jewish in some way, he makes a statement that I've come to understand is a very bold one for a rabbi: 'You should convert!' He offers to tutor me over the Internet—assign me readings and take my questions." Within a year, Michael became a Jew.

Rabbis like the two Michael met, however, are the exception rather than the rule. Some may have the commitment, but not the time. Or the time, but not the personality. Few would offer to tutor a stranger over the Internet and guide him through the conversion process into the Jewish community.

Yet most rabbis believe themselves to be welcoming and open to converts. Alan Silverstein (1995) writes of his rabbinic colleagues, "In each case, Conservative rabbis and congregations will be ready and able to assist you in your quest" (p. xxi). Most are simply unaware of the dual message of openness and rejection that they send by also exclaiming, "Don't date non-Jews!" or promoting conversion only after the quest for endogamous marriage (as defined by birth) fails.

The notion that a conversion should be difficult, like the process of becoming a Jew, is described by a Reform rabbi:

Although I don't do the traditional turning away of somebody three times, my modern application of that is to stress how difficult conversion is. In most cases, it is going to be at least a year. I make it very clear to potential converts that even though we may decide to start the process now, it doesn't mean that we are going to finish the process. Anytime along the way they may decide that it is not for them. I have people who haven't come back after the first meeting, and I had a woman who wanted to go on and get a Conservative conversion.

Another Reform rabbi outlines his plan of study for conversion. It sounds very much like earning a higher degree—an oral exam process—rather than an interesting, enjoyable, and challenging journey:

They have to study, and it is an extended period of study. I require them to attend Shabbat services twice a month for the period of study. . . . They meet with me individually about once a month for six weeks, and we discuss issues and problems and progress. There is a conversion support group for couples that meets monthly when we have enough couples to get a group together. We have been pretty successful with that over the years. It is a good group. Ultimately, they need to join the temple. They need to commit to being part of the Jewish community. Then . . . there is that point where people pass from thinking that they are going to become Jewish and deciding that they are going to become Jewish to feeling Jewish or whatever. They need to get to that point. . . . It usually takes a year or so. They need to write an essay describing their journey into Judaism. We have a *Beit Din* in which we primarily discuss the essay.

If someone inquires about becoming Jewish, rabbis should respond with enthusiasm and encouragement, not with suspicion or challenge. The road to conversion should be laid out clearly, of course, and presented as a desirable pathway, not an obstacle to overcome. Individuals should not have to *prove* that they are interested in Judaism to receive encouragement from a rabbi about possibly becoming a Jew. Rabbis can state unequivocally that it is good for Jews to form Jewish households. Whether the path to Judaism is through birth or conversion, however, must be irrelevant.

This is not to say, of course, that a person who is encouraged to convert to Judaism will do so. Some individuals who marry Jews are hostile to Judaism (or to any organized religion). Some may feel they need time to become familiar and comfortable with the community before considering conversion. Many have to balance familial pressures from their own parents or grandparents not to abandon their non-Jewish upbringing. Still, many non-Jews are open to considering Judaism as their adopted religion, and millions of non-Jews may choose Judaism even if they are not married to a Jew. The attitudes and behaviors of rabbis, as "officials" of Judaism, are a key determinant in bringing the individual or family into Jewish life.

What Rabbis Should Do

Determined or clear-visioned individuals could have the stamina to see more than one rabbi if they are initially turned down or discouraged. Hardier souls might go through the process of talking to a number of rabbis or visiting a number of synagogues (think of Hazel). A bad encounter with a rabbi, however, may sour someone irreparably and permanently.

An unsupportive rabbi can make the journey toward Judaism daunting and unpleasant. One woman, seeking to convert prior to marrying a man who was born Jewish, wrote of her initial steps toward conversion:

> The first rabbi we met discouraged us from pursuing whatever plans we had. . . . I had heard from friends that rabbis will ask you many questions—some negative—to make sure you really want to convert. But I was not happy with his attitude. He came across as very negative and demeaning. Nor did I like how he was viewing our situation. For example, he had Sunday classes in Judaism for potential converts. In our area it is customary for couples to attend the classes together (which Steven and I both wanted to do), but because we had jobs for which Sunday was the most important day, we could not attend them. When we told the rabbi this, he said he felt we were not really serious about converting if we were not willing to commit ourselves to attending Sunday classes. I was upset at how he came to this conclusion, even though we said we would be happy to make special trips anywhere in our area

for classes during the rest of the week. It seemed like a very petty thing upon which to base such a serious remark [Berkowitz and Moskovitz, 1996, pp. 64–65].

Lena Romanoff, founder and director of Jewish Converts and Interfaith Network, (1990) rightly assesses the inescapable and therefore crucial role of the rabbi in pointing out that how the rabbi thinks and behaves should be a cornerstone in any rethinking about conversion policy:

> Whereas a born Jew may not need a rabbi in order to feel Jewish, a convert needs at least one rabbi in order to become Jewish. Since conversion is such an intimate and highly emotional experience, it is little wonder that the rabbis who encounter prospective converts at such a juncture in their lives can significantly influence their entire view of Judaism.
>
> For this reason, the spirit in which conversion is provided is sometimes even more important than the content of a conversion course itself. From an initial call of inquiry made to the rabbi's office to the last day of formal study and beyond, the rabbis encountered by the prospective convert set the tone for that individual's entry into Jewish life. It is an awesome responsibility.
>
> The influence that a rabbi may have on a prospective convert can, of course, be either positive or negative, and sometimes a little of both. First impressions count [p. 147].

Romanoff's prescription for effective rabbinic roles is so comprehensive and logical that it is reprinted here in its entirety:

1. Incorporate hands-on workshops as an integral part of the conversion program. Many converts expressed frustration that when all was said and done, they were unequipped with synagogue skills and unable to light

Shabbat or Hanukkah candles, dress the Torah, put on tefillin, build a Sukkah, make a Seder, or prepare for the holidays.

2. Implement a "buddy system" for converts to attend synagogue services in pairs or small groups. Going to a synagogue alone can be a frightening and lonely experience. Also include in the discussion about synagogues the roles of the rabbi, cantor, and ritual director and how they function in each branch of Judaism as well as how their roles differ from those of priests and ministers.

3. Provide a list of recommended books for converts to buy as well as a Jewish calendar and a list of Jewish places of interest in the community. Converts like to have these for future reference.

4. Match prospective converts with other new Jews or born Jews in the community who are willing to act as hosts. This is especially important for converts who do not have Jewish in-laws or friends who can serve as role models.

5. Arrange visits to Jewish museums, kosher meat markets or bakeries, a *mikvah* (before the actual conversion), a Jewish funeral home, and other places of Jewish interest. If such field trips cannot be arranged with the whole class, host families can help the convert locate these places and provide companionship and explanations during visits.

6. Provide access to qualified professionals and resource people in the Jewish community who can discuss issues of concern such as personal and familial conflicts, divorce, and child rearing. Rabbis should also tell their students when they are available for consultation outside the class setting. Rabbis sometimes assume that students know they are available, but the fact is that many converts say they are reluctant "to bother the busy rabbi."

7. Provide opportunity for discussion of issues relating to families, both Christian and Jewish. In addition, many rabbis avail themselves to both families throughout the conversion process. Those who provide a special session for parents to interact with each other as well as with the rabbi receive special kudos from their converts. Other rabbis, who believe that it is either not appropriate or not their responsibility to get involved with families, leave some converts feeling very frustrated and ill equipped to approach their families on issues of Jewish theology and ritual.

8. Add to the course curriculum (if they are not already included) such topics as the history of conversion and intermarriage, the branches of Judaism, patrilineal and matrilineal descent, and anti-Semitism. Many converts also expressed the desire for some introduction to Jewish culture, including Jewish art, music, dance, and Yiddish. Although the converts understood that time restrictions do not allow for full exploration of these topics, they suggested that reading and resource lists could provide for further study after an initial exposure. Several converts suggested that students be given the opportunity to research and report to the others on subjects not generally discussed in class. Topics beyond those already mentioned could include Soviet Jewry, Jews of other lands, modern Israel, righteous gentiles, as well as Jewish views on homosexuality, AIDS, surrogate motherhood, organ transplants, infertility, and death.

9. Pay special attention to Jewish partners. In general converts would like to see attendance of their Jewish partners in the conversion class made mandatory. If sickness, distance, or work precludes partner participation, there should be a requirement to meet with the converting

rabbi or another rabbi at least three times prior to the conclusion of the program.

10. Invite converts who have become involved in the community to address the class, providing insight into their own conversion experiences and answering questions that other converts may be best equipped to handle.

11. Keep abreast of recent literature and programming on conversion and intermarriage. Refer prospective converts and their families to existing support groups, or, if they don't already exist in a particular area, establish new ones. Three-quarters of the respondents either had access to a support group or expressed the desire to join one. Others who felt they didn't need support groups said they would like to see one available for parents, both Jewish and non-Jewish.

12. Provide a list of synagogues in the area, with a brief description of each. A bit more controversial was the repeated suggestion that converts be provided with free one- or two-year memberships in local synagogues and community centers. Many converts also expressed interest in learning about *Havurot* as an alternative to membership in larger, more established synagogues.

Most of the converts agreed that the ideal length of a conversion course should be a year so that the convert can experience an entire Jewish calendar of events. Many, however, added that they did not have the time or willingness to commit themselves to a year-long conversion. An excellent suggestion was that the program be divided into two six-month periods—the first being mandatory, the second voluntary [pp. 160–162].

Even though many rabbis do *some* of these things, it is the exception rather than the rule for these practices to be widespread in

any community. Given all of their responsibilities, most congregational rabbis find it logistically impossible to give serious attention
to conversion in this way for more than a few individuals at a time.
Most communities do not have many noncongregational rabbis to
engage individuals in conversion.

The Mixed-Marriage Ceremony Controversy

So much controversy has developed about whether or not a rabbi
should perform a mixed-marriage ceremony that a tug of war exists
between the laity and the rabbinate. Indeed, a power play is under
way, with most of the Jewish public demanding that rabbis perform
mixed marriages and most rabbis upholding a different set of standards. The marriage ceremony looms as the major battleground for
intermarriage, more than any other life cycle event or participation
in other Jewish organizations.

The level of anger and frustration is tied to the panic mode for
both institutions and individuals. On the one hand, marrying a
non-Jew is tragic. On the other hand, this is a liberal pluralistic society where people have the option to marry whomever they want.
These extremes cannot be settled in a marriage ceremony. Behaving as if Jewish communal survival rests in the single decision of
who marries a couple can make all the players feel either righ-
teously indignant or else satisfied that they have won some major
battle, but in the end it does not make that much difference. Fifteen minutes after the wedding ceremony, life goes back to normal,
whatever that is. The issues that the Jewish community—and the
couple and the family—have to face prior to the wedding ceremony remain after the wedding. Of course, for some, marriage by
a rabbi may solidify their path toward Judaism. For others, it does
not matter.

One Orthodox rabbi explains his view of mixed-marriage wedding ceremonies in this way:

Nobody throws anyone out [of the synagogue]. I won't perform the wedding—that goes without saying. [But the] person who chooses to marry out—my feeling is that a person who is really involved in the synagogue doesn't make such a choice. If a person chooses to do so, we don't acknowledge the wedding, but we still receive the person with acceptance. We don't throw somebody out. [On the contrary, we hope] there will be a conversion.

Like other aspects of the complex interaction between Jews and non-Jews, discussing the wedding ceremony in terms of stemming the tide of intermarriage leads to mutually false accusations on both sides. Somebody may feel better or worse, somebody's feelings may be spared, the image of the marriage being OK or not OK may be in the forefront for a short while; but rabbis participating in mixed-marriage ceremonies neither open nor close the floodgates to assimilation.

The great debate about rabbinic officiation at weddings of mixed marrieds is a Jewish communal tempest in a teapot. This is not to say that the meaning and symbolism of the wedding are not of great importance to individuals and families who struggle with the religious future of the family, and how the children will be raised. The symbolism generates great emotion. However, as Egon Mayer (1989) reports: "Analysis of data presented in this report suggests that rabbinic officiation at mixed marriages has relatively little, if any, connection to the expressed Jewishness in the family lives of non-Jews married to Jews. Similarly, rabbinic refusal to officiate at mixed marriages seems to have relatively little, if any, connection with large-scale alienation from Jewish attachments" (pp. 7–8).

The wedding-ceremony debate is an exaggerated presence in the discussion of the relationship of Jews to non-Jews. Some rabbis should do it; it may help. Some should not do it. A mix of responses is our best communal strategy.

Rabbis as Leaders for Proactive Conversion

The role of the rabbi should be to provide leadership in a variety of forms. First, the rabbinate has to provide standards concerning conversion. They ultimately have to say which actions are right or wrong—and, just as important, why. That not all rabbis agree and that there are denominational differences is an accepted tenet of American Judaism and fits well within the pluralistic character of American Jews. A variety of options and interpretations are expected since American Judaism is not monolithic and the rabbinate is not a hierarchical authority. A single edict about conversion does not fit the realities of contemporary American Jewish life. On the other hand, rabbis cannot be effective leaders if they are acting only on personal philosophy and belief. Their beliefs and actions must be tied to a greater set of laws and guidelines that have both theological and communal roots and support. The leadership that comes from setting standards must be accompanied by leadership in explaining those standards.

Second, leadership comes through vision. Adherence to standards must not only have historical and theological antecedents; it must also be connected to some greater vision of the future of the Jewish community. Standards must be connected to other sets of actions that move the community forward. The rabbis must say what they will *not* do and what they *will* do to help individuals who are struggling with conflicts associated with conversion. If rabbis are prepared to say, for example, that they will not marry individuals of different religions, then too they must say that they are willing to educate, counsel, and otherwise help to involve the couple as they struggle with issues of dual identity. All actions must be tied to some vision of what the rabbi and the community are attempting to accomplish. In-marriage for its own sake cannot be a singular driving or compelling goal. The standards have to signify some desire for a cohesive and vibrant Jewish community. This is difficult to communicate in times of emotional trauma, but is nevertheless essential.

Finally, rabbis must exert their influence as community activists, within the synagogue and without. If the community is to devise an agenda for building identity and participation, rabbis must be key designers and implementers in the system. They need to build coalitions and direct resources from a vision about what the Jewish community ought to be. They must be proactive in guiding people to what they should do. Arguing against proactive conversion does not provide much leadership or vision; it only puts a negative spin on what it means to be a Jew and induces guilt and anxiety among those who are seeking marriage partners or who have already chosen one who was not born Jewish.

Training Rabbis

Recruiting and training knowledgeable, charismatic rabbis must be at the core of any communal strategy of group survival and growth. Without a strong core of religious leadership, the community of Jews lacks the depth and guidance it requires to prosper in a pluralistic society where there are so many attractive options from which to choose. Judaism needs advocates who can promote the joy and fulfillment of Jewish life. Engaging and well-respected rabbis who act as promoters of Judaism must be recruited and trained to actively encourage individuals to become and remain Jews. These individuals must operate both within the synagogue and outside that context.

Although creating a vibrant rabbinate does not solve the problems of conversion, the converse is true: the Jewish community cannot effectively deal with the issues surrounding conversion without a retrained and rededicated rabbinate. An invigorated rabbinate is no panacea, but little progress is made in the long run without supporting the rabbis who build Jewish life.

Most require new training as community organizers. To have credibility and legitimacy, they need a strong base in Jewish knowledge as well as institution-building skills. They need not be the chief operating officers of their synagogue (often management positions), but rather true moral and ethical teachers, providing vision and leadership instead of micromanaging the synagogue.

What is most needed is a group of rabbis who understand and can navigate the permeable relationship between the Jewish community and the general community. They must be as prepared to attract, encourage, and educate non-Jews to become Jews as they are to teach and lead all Jews. The United States is a whirlwind of denominational switching. Jews become Christians and Buddhists, and vice versa. Individuals switch denominations within religious traditions, moving from Orthodox to Reform or Reconstructionist to Conservative. They do it because they marry someone of another faith or set of practices, or because they are on a personal quest for community or religious purpose. Individuals are in a constant flow of becoming or unbecoming. Like nearly all aspects of American culture, there are a great array of choices open to everyone, and individuals are encouraged to test, experiment, move on, and try something new.

This reality touches both Jews and non-Jews alike. Rabbis must be the representatives who explain, encourage, nurture, promote, reinforce, and attract, keeping existing Jews engaged and bringing in non-Jews. Other religions have proactive, charismatic clergy and laity attempting to bring in converts and adherents. Judaism can do no less, both for those who were born Jews and for those who were not. Rabbis must trumpet Judaism as beneficial to the individual, extol what it does for each person, and proclaim what each person can do for the community. The benefits of ritual, peoplehood, uniqueness, communal bonds, history, and theology must be thoroughly understood and promoted. Being keepers of the faith requires aggressive, positive promotion. More sour statements about history, obligation, suffering, or loss do not hold or attract the next generation of Jews. Judaism has so much more to offer.

The seminaries must develop recruitment guidelines and mechanisms to find such people, who by strength of character, knowledge, charisma, and commitment can be the advocates for Judaism in America's religious marketplace. The Reform and Conservative movements, which include most of America's Jews, have much to learn from Chabad (a Hasidic community), both in message and execution. They shamelessly and aggressively promote Judaism, focusing intently on born Jews.

Rabbis need more courses in comparative religion, building personal relationships, community organizing, and the psychology of organizational change. They have to draw on business, psychology, and a multitude of other disciplines and knowledge bases. They have to learn about community design and planning theory, and about how to be communal and institutional architects. They have to draw on leadership training. They must be the pied pipers of the Jewish community and bring along the non-Jews as well.

Changing the Tone

Individuals struggling with their religious identity cannot respond to implications or threats that they are being bad Jews or bad individuals, or that somehow they are personally responsible for the destruction of Jewish life. Some individuals, of course, condemn rabbis no matter what they do if they disagree with a rabbi's decision that affects them personally. Some people react negatively to establishment of any standards, or if those standards are applied to them as individuals. But most individuals respond with respect and understanding if they feel they have been treated accordingly.

Most of the interaction, therefore, must come at times other than crisis moments in individuals' lives. Rabbis should have frequent opportunities to teach a philosophy of Jewish life to as many individuals as possible. This must take place within and outside the congregational setting. Rabbis need to exert their leadership through positing and inspiring an attractive vision of Jewish life. The issue of conversion is inextricably bound with the overall constructs of the Jewish community and its attractiveness and cohesiveness in the minds of Jews.

The language of tests, exams, job interviews, and obstacles seems very destructive. Rabbis need to be cheerleaders, not prison guards. They need to help unlock the doors and gates, not bar them. They need to present potential converts with smiles and challenges, not frowns and declarations of the improbable, difficult, or unattainable. Rather than ask people to prove why they want to be Jewish, they should advocate for Judaism, explaining why it is good to be a Jew, talking about the positive benefits individually, familially, and communally from a belief in Jewish ideals as a practice of Jewish life, rather than trying to have people prove at the outset of considering conversion that they are interested in these aspects of Judaism, which they know little or nothing about. Rabbis must overcome a host of personal feelings and institutional constraints to promote conversion. They cannot send mixed messages or equivocate. Some rabbis have achieved this success. Their ranks must grow dramatically if the Jewish community is to flourish.

7

The Case for Conversion

The case for conversion is the case for Judaism. We need to promote our unique role as a people. Peoplehood includes ethnic, religious, and national components. All of these components are mutually reinforcing. The religious components include modes of worship, theology, and ritual observance. The ethnic components include language, history, mythology, peer groups, social institutions, and common enemies. Many of the norms and values of the ethnic group are rooted in the theology of Judaism, including promotion of social justice and development of human service networks. The ethnic components of the group are also tied to religious ritual, such as the family celebration of Passover.

Judaism is a religion of action. More than elsewhere, it is *not* the thought that counts. If Jews retain their Jewish "identity" but do not act upon it, then the Jewishness of Judaism is hollow. Jewish identity that is unexpressed through communal involvement is Judaism without warmth or substance. The attractiveness of Judaism is its vibrant activity.

A critical component of Jewish peoplehood is the central place of Israel in the theology and culture of Jews. The state of Israel is embedded deep in the consciousness of Jews. Jewish history has long included the promise and settling of a nation. After Jews were exiled from their home, returned, and exiled again, they spent almost two thousand years preparing to return once more. Jews have achieved their calling to return to Jerusalem only in the past fifty years. Promoting connections to Israel is a vital part of our case.

Jewish theology, ritual observance, social customs, and language have all evolved over the millennia in a variety of ways. There has never been, nor likely ever will be, any single, authentic Judaism. We have no pope, catechism, or theological tribunal (ultra-Orthodox claims to authority in Israel notwithstanding). Liturgy, ritual observance, and social interaction all change and evolve over time, and there has been tremendous latitude and variety among Jewish cultures in different times and places, constant reinterpretation and adjustment. New ideas and practices invariably dot the Jewish landscape. Beliefs and activities come and go, institutions are created and abandoned, great bodies of knowledge consistently added to and reconfigured. Various levels of Orthodox, Conservative, Reform, Reconstructionist, and other denominations add to the richness of the landscape of Jewish life. Each has something to say and something legitimate to offer.

The community needs to emphasize accomplishments that have been met and progress that has been made. We should not dwell on what we do not do on the personal level. We should deemphasize all the ways in which an individual is not successful in observance, practice, and participation. Recognition of accomplishments is more productive than shame over one's religious failures. Building a positive identity must offer joy and satisfaction. It is sad that most personal interviews with Jews reveal individuals lamenting or excusing their own self-assessment that they are not "religious Jews"; their admission reveals a sense of inauthenticity and failure. Often, these individuals belong to synagogues, have been involved in social justice activities all their lives, are very active in performing *mitzvot*, and feel only positive about being Jewish. Yet they are apologetic, ashamed, or regretful that they are not "better" Jews. This is often the message of the Jewish institutional structure: it is never enough, no matter what you do.

If the task of being a better Jew seems so daunting, if expectations are so high, if the risk of failure is so immense, then many Jews end up shrugging their shoulders. They feel guilt and remorse, but not enough to alter their lives in ways they believe will not lead to success anyway. "So you go to synagogue once a month; it should be twice a month. Or every week. During the week. Twice a day. Be available for a minyan. If you observe Shabbat, pray and have a respite from the work week. No. Watch the light switches." Someone is always setting standards that are beyond someone else's. It makes many Jews give up before they start.

The Jewish community needs more venues for people to express their religious beliefs so that much of the good that they do is defined as being a good Jew, rather than segregating the goodness of their lives from the Jewishness of their lives. Individuals choose to opt out because in their minds they have little choice whether to live as Americans or live as good Jews. We should abandon the norms that say no matter what someone does it is not enough. How can the Jewish community possibly include others and help them feel part of Jewish life if even born Jews are made to feel that they are inauthentic (whatever that means) unless they attend synagogue every week, strictly observe *kashrut*, and *daven* every day?

Jewish history is long, and Jews who promote "authentic" Judaism are selective about which period and which place they draw upon. Jewish history did not begin in the sixteenth century. Judaism's beliefs, ritual practice, custom, and institutional structures do not need to be the Judaism of preemancipation Eastern Europe. We are eclectic and differentiated. That is a strength.

Those who represent Judaism cannot talk about the burdensome responsibilities of being Jews; quite the opposite. The joys of Torah, the rewards of living a Jewish life, the sense of accomplishment that comes through responsibility is what must be represented. Judaism cannot be portrayed as something sour that one has to swallow, but rather something bold, innovative, and unique as a religious faith tradition. Jews cannot approach conversion with a "so why would anybody want to be Jewish" attitude or insist that someone become Jewish just because their parents or grandparents were. It must have a rationale and demonstrated usefulness within the family construct.

Who Advocates for Conversion?

The advocates for proactive conversion are few and far between in the rabbinic, scholarly, and lay communities. The first major rabbinic figure in the past generation to approach the subject was Rabbi Alexander Schindler, who, as head of the Reform movement in 1979, openly called for proselytizing among non-Jews. Schindler's call for proactive conversion is still powerful and inspiring: "But we live in America today. No repressive laws restrain us. The fear of persecution no longer inhibits us. There is no earthly reason now why we cannot reassume our ancient vocation and open our arms wide to all newcomers. Why are we so hesitant? Are we ashamed? Must one really be a madman to choose Judaism? Let us shuffle off our insecurities! Let us recapture our self-esteem! Let us demonstrate our confidence in those worths which our faith enshrines!" (in Epstein, 1995, p. 77).

Some Jews dismissed Schindler because he led the Reform movement, which consistently outpaced itself in the Jewish community. The Reform movement was far ahead of the rest of the organized Jewish community in at least paying conceptual attention to the concept of outreach. At a minimum, Reform leaders promoted institutional recognition that mixed marriage was a communal reality and some efforts had to be made to deal with it.

A generation earlier, some called for proactive conversion. As early as 1949, Leo Baeck advocated a missionary effort on the part of Jews, recalling the success of Islam, Buddhism, and Christianity in doing so. In a 1949 address to the World Union for Progressive Judaism, he said:

A place for missionaries must be established. We can no longer live without it. We would not see the signs of the times without seeing this. Our self-esteem, our self-respect ask it of us. The Jews of America can do it. They must do it. Here also their honour is engaged, not the one at the cost of the other, but both belong together. . . . One thing is necessary, one question stands before us. Our destiny puts this question. Are we great enough for it? We must have great thoughts, we must begin to think highly, nobly, magnanimously. All depends on great ideas. One is inclined often to say: let anybody think what he may, if only he thinks in a great manner, if only the thoughts he thinks are great, noble thoughts. That is the future [1995, p. 13].

Only a great vision of what Judaism can and should be fulfills the mission of being a light unto the nations.

Schindler and Baeck had some ideological support. In *Conversion to Judaism: From the Biblical Period to the Present*, Rabbi Joseph R. Rosenbloom (1978) traces the history of conversion and proselytizing. A reform rabbi in St. Louis and adjunct professor of classics at Washington University, he documents how conversion has helped Jews survive and grow over the millennia: "Conversion to Judaism served the survival needs of the Jewish group throughout history. While official and popular attitudes on proselytizing occasionally were out of harmony with actual practice, ideology usually caught up with the practices demanded by necessity. When peoples do not survive, it is clear that they responded inadequately or not at all to the challenges facing them. Just the opposite is the case when they do survive. Conversion was one of the major survival tools invented and repeatedly used by Jews" (p. 142).

He also makes the case that promoting Judaism as a religion, theology, or way of life is a positive contribution to civilization as a whole. He says that promoting Judaism should be viewed not only as a survival technique but as an enriching gift Jews have to offer a troubled and often spiritually scarred world:

Yet there may be a special role for Judaism in the West, where the secular religions of scientism, nationalism, communism, as well as others, have not been complete successes. Great numbers of people feel a lack in their lives which they vaguely describe as spiritual. Religions based on man's depravity and on mythic salvation schemes do not seem to contain an answer to such cravings. Judaism, however, particularly where it expresses its belief in man's potential and fosters his fulfillment both sensuously and intellectually, may provide such an answer. To accomplish this Judaism must take a few steps forward from the closed medievalism it still retains, and which produces its enclavist and ghetto outlook on life, and several steps backward to those ancient attitudes which were outward-looking in their encouragement for seeking and winning converts [p. 145].

Harold Schulweis, a Conservative rabbi with an impeccable reputation as a thinker and doer in that movement, also supports proactive conversion. He exhorts American Jews to begin active conversion efforts for unaffiliated Christians. An April 1997 article in *Moment* magazine titled "Seek Converts!" outlined his call for the Jewish community to openly embrace proselytizing and proactive conversion within the Jewish community. Schulweis effectively argues that both Abraham and Sarah were converts to Judaism:

Why not open our arms to those who seek a spiritual way of life? Are we not told in the classic text of Avoth DeReppe Nathan (2ba) that Jews are urged to bring people beneath the wings of the divine presence exactly as Abraham and Sarah had done? . . . The logic is clear and so is the theology. Judaism is not an exclusive club of born Jews. It is a universal faith with an ancient tradition that has deep resonance for people today. . . . And, unfortunately, the ideas of choice and conversion upset some Jews because they feel Judaism is less an ideology than a biology, a matter of chromosomes, not choice [pp. 43–44].

Schulweis calls the genetic predisposition ideology what it is: a form of prejudice. He says, "Bias against converts blocks a national, even international, Jewish movement to educate, invite, and embrace non-Jews. We are paying a terrible price for all that prejudice. If Judaism is a world religion, then it has something valuable to offer the world" (p. 45).

As reported in the *Jewish Bulletin of Northern California*, "Orthodox and Conservative rabbis have taken issue with Schulweis, saying that Jews must first focus on the indifferent and unaffiliated in their own ranks before trying to attract non-Jews" (Tugend, 1996, p. 25). In the same article, Rabbi Raphael Butler, national executive vice president of the Orthodox Union, argues that "millions of Jews have responded to an aggressive outreach campaign, while proselytizing non-Jews would be seen as a sign of weakness" (p. 25). Rabbi Malcolm Sauer, head of graduate Judaic studies at the Yeshiva of Los Angeles, repeats the interpretation that Jewish law requires that would-be converts "be discouraged and pushed away rather than courted" (p. 25). Given the common argument about scarce resources, Rabbi William Lebeau, dean of the Rabbinical School and Jewish Theological Seminary in New York, declares: "We have to decide whether to use our limited resources and energy on reaching non-Jews, or within the Jewish community including the intermarried" (p. 25).

Vince Beiser, in an article for the *Jerusalem Report*, found that few community leaders were ready to embrace Schulweis's call for a new approach to issues of conversion, but he did identify a few allies. Beiser summarizes well the overall Jewish community's attitudes toward conversion: "Still, few prominent Jewish religious leaders besides Schulweis support the idea of actually going out and encouraging conversion, except in cases of intermarriage. From ultra-Orthodox Hasidim to Reform Jews, everyone favors opening the door into Judaism if someone finds their own way to it and knocks loud and long enough; but almost no one wants to put up signs on the lawn inviting people in" (1997, p. 30).

One of the best essays on the merits of conversion was written by Dennis Prager in a 1995 article titled, "Judaism Must Seek Converts." He captures the myriad reasons why it would be good for the Jews to seek converts and outlines many of the reasons that Jews do not currently engage in open conversion. He argues that increasing the number of Jews is important because it would reduce anti-semitism by tying Jews more to other populations. He also argues that more non-Jews are open to Judaism than born Jews because they do not carry the negative baggage that many born Jews have from their poor or almost nonexistent upbringing as Jews:

> Unlike many born Jews, untold numbers of non-Jews would love to be part of the Jewish people and live a Jewish life. They would love a religion that stresses right behavior over right faith, that teaches one how to incorporate the holy into everyday life, that stresses a life of the intellect, that makes one a member of a people as well as a religion, that is the oldest ongoing civilization in the world, that gave the world God and the Ten Commandments, and that, through involvement with the Jewish people, keeps one passionately involved in the great moral issues of the day—from the Middle East to Eastern Europe to relations with Christians and Moslems [p. 89].

He makes a strong case that new blood adds a great deal to Jewish life, to how we think and feel and act. New advocates bring new ideas: "Jews by choice bring something else into Jewish life—freshness. We have become too inbred, too much like each other (even when we thoroughly dislike each other). New Jews bring healthy attitudes toward Judaism, toward the world. True, they don't come with childhood memories of Shabbat, but neither do the vast majority of born Jews anymore, and they also don't come with unhealthy Jewish emotional baggage from childhood. They bring an attitude of joy of being Jewish, not just the 'shver zu sein a Yid' ('It's tough to be a Jew') attitude that many Jews have" (pp. 87–88).

Prager also argues that the world would be a much better place if so many individuals were practicing Judaism: "Imagine a world in which a hundred million Jews were trying to lead lives in accordance with Jewish values. Imagine a world that set aside its preoccupation with money one day each week. Imagine a society in which tens of millions of its members really believed that gossiping was wrong, where a sex ethic lying between hedonism and sexual repression became the norm, where people consulted Jewish laws before entering business deals. Imagine a world that read Isaiah weekly, that studied biblical and other Jewish texts a few hours each week during office hours" (p. 87).

Continuous opposition to conversion is so odd, since most people agree that converts make good Jews. The tribal reluctance is difficult to overcome, but some of us are starting to promote the benefits of dedicated converts:

> Around the country, there is no doubt that a certain consciousness and awareness has been raised within the Jewish community. This has allowed many intermarried couples to find a niche, and has allowed many Jews-by-choice to be regarded with new eyes by heretofore skeptical Jews. . . . "I am positive about the future. We are gaining converts who are educated, intelligent and excited," says UAHC facilitator Robin Farquhar, whose mid-Atlantic region covers 62 Reform congregations in Delaware, Maryland, Virginia, West Virginia and North Carolina. . . . Many rabbis note the enthusiasm and energy that Jewish converts bring to their communities. Rabbi Allen Kensky, who served Beth Israel Congregation, a

Conservative synagogue in Ann Arbor, Mich., for 17 years
before joining the faculty of the Jewish Theological Seminary,
notes that Jews-by-choice were among the most dedicated
and active members of the culturally diverse college town's
Jewish community [Benson, 1992, p. 75].

Egon Mayer and Carl Sheingold (1979) summarize the positive
effects of conversion and the negative effects of neglect:

> The findings summarized above tend to reinforce the fear that
> intermarriage represents a threat to Jewish continuity. Most
> non-Jewish spouses do not convert to Judaism; the level of
> Jewish content and practice in mixed marriages is low; only
> about one-third of the Jewish partners in such marriages view
> their children as Jewish; and most such children are exposed
> to little by way of Jewish culture or religion. Thus, despite the
> suggestions of some Jews that intermarriage may actually add
> to the Jewish population by bringing non-Jewish spouses and
> the children of such unions into the Jewish fold, this study—
> conducted with a sample that made optimistic conclusions
> more likely—does not support this hope. It does, however, sug-
> gest steps the Jewish community might take to ameliorate the
> assimilationist threat inherent in intermarriage.
>
> One set of data—the findings on conversionary marriages—
> merits particular attention and discussion. Conversionary mar-
> riages compare favorably not only with mixed marriages, but
> with endogamous marriages as well. In the conversionary mar-
> riage, Jewish identity is not merely asserted; it is acted upon,
> particularly with respect to religious affiliation and observance.
> Thus, in some ways, there is more reason for optimism about
> Jewish continuity in families where the born-Gentile spouse
> has converted to Judaism than there is in the typical endoga-
> mous family [p. 30].

Identity Transformation:
How Does Conversion Really Take Place?

The need for a new language to discuss the process and act of becoming a Jew is compelling. We shall discuss conversion as transformation. An individual does not convert from one state to another; identity transforms through both experience and understanding. The transformed identity leads to inclusion, a sense of belonging. Ruth did not convert; she became a Jew. The concept of *becoming* is vital, especially since the process begins prior to formal declarations and continues afterward.

Identity transformation and becoming must take place in two realms. The first is promoting *religious* conversion. This is the process where individuals become part of Judaism as a religion by understanding its laws, its forms of worship, its ritual observance, and so on. Most discussions of conversion focus on religious conversion. The Jewish community must also combine active promotion of religious conversion with *communal* conversion as well. Communal conversion takes place through the adoptions and values and norms of the Jewish people, their customs in terms of language, history, mythology, self-views, and institutional participation.

Sometimes a Jew helps create another Jew. The process also works in reverse. A Jew with a marginal Jewish identity, but one that he or she is unwilling to abandon completely, may marry someone who has deep religious and spiritual convictions and who is willing to transfer those convictions to Judaism. If given venues for expression and encouragement, the non-Jewish spouse's interest in Judaism may become more involved and more passionate than that of the Jewish spouse. The "new Jew" can bring the Jewish partner and the children along, facilitating the process of identity transformation for born Jews as well as for himself or herself.

One of the most powerful paths to identity transformation is through a passionate and committed Jewish spouse. Jews who believe deeply and understand their religious beliefs and practices can teach their non-Jewish spouses through their own practice.

This is why the prevention strategy is so insulting. It assumes that the non-Jew is something to be prevented, or fought against, when individuals not born Jewish may bring more interest, enthusiasm, and passion to Judaism than a born Jew. Indeed, the energy of a new Jew may be the best mode of intervention to motivate the born Jew to actually become involved in Jewish life. An enthusiastic Jew-by-inclusion may have more influence on a nonpracticing, distant, or nonbelieving Jew than do parents, grandparents, siblings, and synagogues combined. The person one sleeps with may have more opportunities for intervention and influence than the rabbi's sermon on Rosh Hashanah or the distant influence of the day school one attended when eleven years old.

The act of becoming a Jew is really a process with final actions that include ritual ceremonies declaring that an individual has become part of the Jewish people. The process of actually becoming a Jew involves a wide range of activities leading to identity transformation. Identity transformation is adoption of one identity and abandonment of another. Becoming part of the Jewish people means accepting, to one degree or another, the Jewish experience as one's own, as well as cultural attitudes and norms, religious practices, and membership in a community's groups and institutions. It involves adopting a Jewish perspective, from a myriad of options, in debates or disagreements. Identity transformation means thinking and feeling like a Jew and feeling bound to the community of Jews, for better or worse.

The process of identity transformation can take place in a number of ways. One path is through study, learning, and education, a cognitive approach that involves absorbing knowledge and sets of ideas. Acquiring this knowledge comes through formal and informal channels, studying texts, and secondary sources, and also through lectures, conversation, and various media. The learning process includes history, theology, the sociology and behavior of the contemporary Jewish community, language, and a host of other elements that make up community. It includes both the religious and the cultural aspects of the Jewish people and can be learned in individual study, classes, and participation in institutions such as synagogues, Jewish community centers, or the United Jewish Appeal. It also comprises elements of worship, volunteerism, philanthropy, and customs and norms relating to holidays and life cycle events such as marriage, birth, and death.

Another path of identity transformation may be within the context of a relationship before marriage, during marriage, or through friendships. Individuals who become part of Jewish families and are exposed to Jewish culture and ritual may find it attractive and fulfilling. This transformation may also take place for a person growing up in a Jewish neighborhood (there are still some) and having primarily Jewish friends or a Jewish best friend.

The motivations for becoming a Jew also differ. They include, among others, selecting a Jewish spouse, searching for spiritual well-being, or desiring to be part of a vibrant community. The length of time, too, varies a great deal. Identity transformation may take place quickly, for example through some cataclysmic event in one's life, or because at some point in time the motivation is incredibly strong to become part of a Jewish family. Or years might transpire as a person is gradually immersed in Jewish life, usually through marriage. Identity transformation through friendship, as one begins to think and act like a Jew, perhaps unintentionally, can take years.

The starting points for transformation differ as well. One may begin the process of becoming a Jew through religious dimensions first, that is, learning how to worship, studying theology, and learning how to observe religious rituals. Or one's induction into Jewish life might be primarily cultural: belonging to a Jewish community center, visiting the state of Israel, or living in a Jewish neighborhood. All of these, and many more, are entry points into Jewish peoplehood. A person's reason for entering may not be that person's reason for continuing. It is possible that the process begins as an

intellectual decision, or a willful choice because of a marriage partner, and ends up being a very emotional odyssey as one is swept
away in a newfound identity. Conversely, one might live within
Jewish environments for a long period of time and already believe
oneself to be part of the Jewish community, and begin intellectual
pursuit of learning the hows and whys of Judaism well after feeling
a major connection.

Because becoming a Jew has many possible starting points and
no prescribed time limit, it is unlikely that most individuals who
marry Jews decide to become a Jew before a marriage ceremony.
Most are neither intellectually nor emotionally committed enough,
immersed enough yet in the community of Jews to understand what
it means to become a Jew. This is especially so if the Jewish partners are younger, are less affiliated, and possess marginal Jewish
knowledge themselves. Many young people are unable to initiate
the acculturation process for a non-Jewish mate or potential mate
because they themselves are ignorant of or dubious about their own
Jewish identity. They are not sure what it means to be a Jew and
therefore are unable to convey to a potential marriage partner
much about Judaism or what it means to become part of the Jewish community. Furthermore, there are practically no support services to help young people engage in the process of teaching about
Judaism. Since many Jewish organizations and agencies are not
very hospitable to non-Jews, the acculturation process is difficult
to commence.

The Marriage-Religion Continuum: Identity
Transformation Within a Marriage

In the past, the rules about defining Judaism through marriage and
birth were much simpler. Jews and non-Jews alike almost always
knew whether someone was in or out. Marrying a non-Jew would
often mean becoming part of the non-Jewish world. Most individuals did not attempt to live Jewish lives married to non-Jews; they

were out. Some individuals, mainly women, converted to Judaism; they were in, part of the Jewish community—even if Jews remained wary or concerned about them. Still, the marriage landscape remained largely uncluttered. Now, all of this has changed, including the family construct. It is unclear today what a Jewish household is and is not. Even two born Jews may be far removed from Jewish community involvement, and this is just the least confusing aspect. The situation clouds further as we move along the marriage-religion continuum in the United States.

In-marriage signifies the marriage of two Jews who were both born of Jewish parentage. A second configuration is *conversionary* marriage, or a born Jew marrying someone who was not born Jewish but who formally converts to Judaism. *Mixed* marriage signifies a couple with a person born Jewish who is married to someone who was not born Jewish and has not converted to Judaism formally or informally.

In terms of understanding identity transformation, these distinctions are important, especially where children are involved. The focus on the future centers on the religious upbringing and identity of children, in in-married and mixed-married families. Perpetuation of any set of beliefs and behaviors rests in the mechanisms to influence and mold the next generation of adherents and participants. It is often assumed that the children of in-married Jews will be Jews no matter what, because of birth, and that mixed-married children will drift away from Judaism. In either case however, the children can be highly identified or minimally identified as Jews, and this status can change over time.

Communal involvement, ritual practice, and identity as a Jew may all vary within marriage types. A mixed-married family may be more involved in Jewish life than an in-married family. For the most part, mixed marrieds are more on the periphery. This is not a universal characteristic, however, and we need not accept it as immutable.

As the twentieth century closes, hundreds of thousands of Jews have married non-Jews and become parents to hundreds of thousands of children. There are millions of Americans with a Jewish heritage.

The number of converts has also grown somewhat, despite all the barriers. Egon Mayer has studied and written more about intermarriage than any other scholar of contemporary Jewish life. In the article "Why Not Judaism?" Mayer (1991b) traces the growth of converts as a percentage of the Jewish population. He found it was no more than 1 percent until the 1970s, when it grew to 3 percent, its current level. He predicts that by the year 2010, even with no changes in how the Jewish community approaches conversion, converts will constitute 7–10 percent of the population.

Understanding the variations within mixed marriages is vital to a proactive approach to conversion. Some individuals operate on a continuum of change moving toward conversion, while others drift into or actually adopt other religions, and still others move in neither direction.

Mixed marriages are not monolithic; there are three kinds. The first includes a non-Jew who practices Judaism, even though he or she has not formally declared Judaism to be his or her faith by self-definition or through ritual ceremony. This individual may attend synagogue, participate in Shabbat, and celebrate Passover without crossing whatever threshold is necessary to declare oneself to be a Jew, either to oneself or to the Jewish community. Indeed the individual might even say, "I feel Jewish and act Jewish, but I am not a Jew." Conversely he or she may even claim to be a Jew without having gone through formal ritual conversion.

The second category of mixed marriage is a non-Jewish spouse who practices no religion. He or she may attend an occasional holiday celebration such as Passover with the Jewish part of the family, or attend a Christmas dinner with the non-Jewish part of the family, but not believe in any organized religion nor feel like a member of any religious faith. These individuals are often self-proclaimed nonbelievers in God, organized religion, or theology of any kind. Sometimes they practice no religion because they are caught between their spouse's desire to have a Jewish family and the desire not to displease their own parents or grandparents if Christianity, Islam,

or some other religion is important to their extended family. Therefore, they choose religious neutrality so as not to offend anyone.

In the third kind of mixed marriage, the non-Jewish spouse practices another religion. He or she actively believes in Christ or Allah,
for example, attends church, and observes Christian or other religious
practices. The first two categories of mixed marriage are more prevalent than this one, with most non-Jewish spouses either practicing no
religion or being involved with Judaism to some degree or another.
They are prime candidates for long-term identity transformation.

What Happens with the Children When a Jew Marries a Non-Jew?

Conversion does matter in the identity of a Jewish household and
in the ultimate religious identity of the children. For example, an
American Jewish Committee study in 1979 showed the major influence of conversion:

> *Children of Intermarriage* confirmed that, in certain respects,
> there were significant differences between the children of con-
> versionary marriages and the others. If the Gentile-born par-
> ent adopted Judaism, the children in the family were more
> likely than not to consider themselves Jewish and value the
> identification. If there was no parental conversion, it was
> highly unlikely that the children would identify as Jews. Sim-
> ilarly, children of conversionary marriages were more likely to
> receive an intensive Jewish education, celebrate bar or bat
> mitzvah, and observe Jewish holidays than children who had
> one Jewish and one Gentile parent. And when the offspring
> in the sample married, the rate of intermarriage for those
> whose non-Jewish parent had converted matched that of the
> general Jewish population—a little over one-third—while the
> overwhelming majority of the children of mixed-religion cou-
> ples took non-Jewish partners ["Intermarriage," 1986, p. 2].

This study was corroborated by a similar report by a Brandeis University team (Fishman, Rimor, Tobin, and Medding, 1990).

Proactive conversion must acknowledge variations within families over time. Parents may say that they are raising their children in more than one religion, which signifies that they celebrate Christmas and Hanukkah, Easter and Passover, for example, but have no other religious affiliation or training. Or it may mean that one parent actively takes the child to synagogue while the other parent actively takes the child to church. The range of difference between the levels of actual religious participation and how often the parents say they are raising the child in more than one religion also can vary over time. The child may be baptized into one religion, for example, and this may be the last Christian ritual in which the family participates. The children may then participate in Jewish life throughout the rest of their childhood. The child may have a *brit*—a ritual circumcision ceremony—and then participate only in church-related activities in later periods of life. Raising the child in more than one religion usually means not doing very much of anything, since the conflicts between active religious participation in more than one theology or religious community are usually too much for the parents to handle.

The third possibility is for the child to be raised without religion. The family does not belong to any church or synagogue, they do not actively participate in any Jewish ritual or Christian ritual, and sometimes they proclaim disbelief in organized religion or in God. Sometimes the children are raised in no religion because the parents cannot agree in which religion to raise the children, so the parents compromise and do nothing. This sometimes seems the least offensive path for the husband and wife to pursue.

Sometimes the children are raised in a religion other than Judaism, with no Jewish affiliation whatsoever. These are rarer cases in marriages between Jews and non-Jews. Studies show a small percentage of parents raising their children only as Christians or Muslims, for example, with no Jewish upbringing. Few Jews are willing to abandon their identity so completely. In making these choices, many Jews leave the gates open for their spouses and their children to be Jews. They make millions of microdecisions that amount to a de facto continuum of identity transformation and opportunities for family members to become Jews. Without institutional support or religious approval, most Jews in mixed-married families have declared, "I am still a Jew and nothing else."

The gates to Judaism are open because family status and religious identity are so fluid. It is no longer to be assumed that everyone marries once, and that is that. Children's religious upbringing is complicated by the large number of individuals who marry more than once. The spouses may both be Jewish in the first marriage, for example, but one may not be Jewish in the second or third marriage. The reverse may be true, with a biological parent who is Jewish but a stepparent who is not. Because of joint custody, or a switch in custody in one period of a child's life or another, children may be raised by one parent as a Jew when the first marriage is intact, in both religions when the child is with the birth father and stepmother, and then switch back again if yet another marriage or household configuration occurs. In-marriage and mixed marriage may intertwine to weave the most complex configurations. Who is in and who is out in these scenarios?

The more complicated the landscape, the more blurred the issues of identity and participation become. Which influence is more important: that of the parent with whom the child lives, or of one birth parent, or of the stepparents, or of the grandparents? Increasingly, families have to cope with the issue of how to raise their children in terms of religious identity in a much confused landscape.

One of the parental options, of course, is to let the child choose. This takes place within both in-married and mixed-married families. A nonobservant pair of Jews may let their children decide whether or not to have a Jewish education, attend synagogue, or participate in Jewish life in any way. Very often, of course, the children opt not to do so because it is something they do not understand—an added burden in their lives. In mixed-married households, parents who are unresolved often say they will teach their children about a number of religions and let them choose. This is an unfair demand to put on any child. Which religion the child chooses may be tied to how the child feels about a particular parent. One may choose Christianity because he or she identifies with mom, whom the child likes, and reject Judaism because it is identified with the father, who is disliked, or vice versa.

Letting a child choose his or her religious faith tradition is usually more a result of the parents' inability to resolve their own issues than a true intellectual exercise in comparative religion. These same parents, of course, might not let their children choose what school they go to, what clothes they wear, or even what food they eat. The decision, then, to let them choose their religion is more of an opting out and an inability to resolve a deep division between the parents. And what if children want to please both parents? The decision to choose one religion can seem to the child to be tantamount to rejection of the other parent. The only option, therefore, is to choose no religion at all. Most of all, these interactions reveal the deep inability of the community to cope with changes. Help is clearly needed to address these issues. The Jewish community offers little comfort and support.

The Benefits of Inclusion

Reaching out to non-Jews requires the Jewish community to have its house in order, to have strong institutional and programmatic venues and the ability to absorb hundreds of thousands, and then millions, of new individuals. The growth should be strategically planned over time to ensure that the Jewish community can handle all these newcomers in terms of physical space, communal infrastructure, and so on. Growth can be as difficult to manage as decline. But the possibility of being overwhelmed by growth should not deter the community from engaging in growth activities. Rather, it should inspire careful plans for the successes to be achieved.

The case for growth through inclusion can be seen in Figure 7.1. The benefits to the Jewish people of strategies for inclusion can be enormous. Many kinds of growth occur. It may lead to a great renaissance in Jewish life. The first type of growth is ideological. Even embarking on strategies for inclusion takes Jews into a new conceptual realm. By definition, reaching out to others is itself a change in the mind-set of the Jewish community. Success in doing so forces Jews to incorporate new ideas. Judaism has always been adoptive and adaptive. It has survived because it holds to particular traditions and beliefs but is constantly open to interpretation, absorbing elements from various cultures. Different ideas and practices are incorporated. Ideological growth also comes from having to make a clearer statement to the outside world of who Jews are. To attract others, Jews have to be able to say that this is what Judaism is and this is what Jewish peoplehood is about.

Ideological growth is accompanied by growth in participation of more individual Jews, adding richness to the fabric of Jewish life. Those who were born Jewish must be able to articulate the importance of being Jewish and have a strong base from which to teach about Judaism. They have to learn more themselves to explain Judaism to others. Perhaps the greatest incentive to learn about Judaism is the need and desire to explain with knowledge, confidence, and passion what it means to be a Jew to someone who was not born Jewish. This can happen in the context of a relationship between a non-Jew and a Jew, or with friends, colleagues, or even strangers. As Jews reach out to others, they must have something meaningful and important to say.

Those who choose to be included in Jewish life and who were not born Jews come from a position of open choice. They are involved because they want to be and can embrace Judaism with enthusiasm and passion. The entire organizational and institutional structure of Jewish life—synagogues, Jewish community centers, the family structure—can be infused with a sense of energy as the Jewish community fills with participants who want to be part of Jewish

Figure 7.1. The Case for Growth Through Inclusion

Ideology New ideas and clearer vision	**Participation in Jewish Life** Born Jews who are inspired to participate New adherents with positive energy
Institutional Restructuring Redesigned and revitalized institutions	
Intergroup Relations Ability to relate to other ethnic and religious groups	**Religious Depth** Greater knowledge and meaning
Increased Population	**Ability to Repair the World**

people. These individuals have no negative familial or institutional baggage about Judaism. Because they have come from other faith traditions or none at all, they can ask probing questions and push individual Jews to think more about what it means to be a Jew. They bring into Jewish life what has worked (and what has failed) from other faith traditions and institutional venues. In this sense, Jewish organizational and institutional life is somewhat insulated and tends to work within its own conventions rather than looking outward for new ideas. An infusion of new individuals who come from outside the Jewish community brings along their experience and knowledge to help build institutional strength inside the Jewish community.

The third benefit is rebuilding the institutional structure. Institutions that are designed for inclusion thrive because they offer a vehicle for Jews to express their Judaism. Jews making other Jews are a vital part of the Jewish institutional network. We must develop the apparatus to help train people to train others to be Jews; we must teach them to teach and create a network of open doors, available information, and assistance to those who want to be included in the Jewish community. This new institutional network can be a growth enterprise. Aside from the dimension of institutional restructuring as the Jewish community grows, the community has to expand all of the elements that help people be Jews, including education, ritual practice, social advocacy, and so on.

Cooperative mechanisms between institutions have to be developed to carry out this enterprise. New and exciting activities within the Jewish community develop because of the energy and ideas introduced into Jewish life. Some organizations and institutions will probably cease to exist because they outlive their usefulness in a growing and vibrant Jewish community. Growth within new enterprises means pruning of other enterprises. Nothing could be healthier for the institutional structure of the Jewish community.

A fourth benefit of inclusion comes from the enhanced religious depth of those who participate in Judaism. Many who come through the doors do so because they are interested in the theology, religiosity, ritual practice, and meaning of Jewish life. They do not consider these elements of Judaism to be a burden, but rather something new and exciting that provides meaning and structure in life. Those who come from different faith traditions, who believe in God, understand and appreciate worship, and have engaged in ritual practice can make the transfer because they already have some adherence to these components of religion. Those who are disaffected or dissatisfied with their current religious tradition or their current theology can embrace Judaism with deep commitment. This is already evident in the Jewish community from those who have converted to Judaism. They are often more interested and enthusiastic than those who were born Jews. For those who do not come from a religious faith tradition, the concepts of seasonal holidays, Shabbat, and a religion that promotes social action and justice have tremendous appeal. The powerful attraction of Judaism is strengthened if religiosity is integrated into positive aspects of family and community. Social and cultural ideologies help the individual feel positive about the larger world. Because Judaism has so much to offer, the new adherents often have a deep sense of satisfaction that they have chosen to be Jews.

A fifth benefit of encouraging non-Jews to become Jews is the increased ability of Jews to relate to other groups. As more kinds of people become Jews, the racial, ethnic, and national characteristics of the Jewish people change. A successful effort of inclusion results in much larger numbers of Asian, Hispanic, and Black individuals becoming Jews. Significant numbers of Asians in the United States are Christian, and a growing number of Black Americans are Muslim. Religion crosses racial and ethnic backgrounds. Indeed, Judaism has included those of Sephardic as well as Ashkenazi background, for example. A significant minority population of Ethiopian Jews live in Israel. Racial and ethnic diversity adds tremendous richness to the fabric of Jewish life, a rainbow with a beauty all its own. Just as important, in this way the issue of Jews relating to Blacks or other racial groups becomes increasingly irrelevant since Blacks are Jews and Jews are Blacks. How inspiring it would be to have hundreds of synagogues filled with Black, Asian, and Hispanic worshipers and having a diverse Jewish community working together on behalf of social justice in the United States and around the world. Bridging the gap to other groups becomes much simpler if the chief spokespeople for the Jewish people share the part of the heritage of the members of those groups.

New Jews bring to the Jewish community knowledge of worshiping Allah or Christ, participation in other rituals, the mythologies of other groups, and their customs. These experiences remain part of their identity and make their choice to be Jewish even more powerful. These memories are not erased, but the person's commitment to Judaism is even stronger for understanding other faith traditions and choosing to follow instead the laws of Judaism. The new Jews can also pass this knowledge on to their children. The mystery and excitement of Christmas may be much less appealing to the children of converts who can say "I have lived that life, here is what it was like, and I have chosen to be Jewish instead." Or they can demystify Scientology, Buddhism, or any other faith tradition to those around them. Jewish life emphasizes acquiring knowledge;

learning about Judaism is one key to Judaism's survival. Acquiring knowledge may also include understanding other religions, not only through study but through experience.

The sixth benefit is that the size of the Jewish population grows by hundreds of thousands—and hopefully by millions. This growth comes from the continued choice by non-Jews to become Jews and the exponential growth of a population of eight million or fifteen million producing at natural birth rates—as compared to a population of five-and-a-half million. It is difficult to say what the optimal size of the Jewish community should be. A Jewish population that does not grow shrinks in proportion to a world population that continues to mushroom. Of course, more bodies by themselves, if they are not committed to Judaism, are not important to the quality of Jewish life. But having more individuals in the community can bring energy, diversity, enthusiasm, and religion that is alive. Efforts to increase Jewish numbers can be predicated on mechanisms and practices such that the Jews who do enter Jewish life have all of these attributes. This is the direct benefit of proactive conversion.

The need for a critical mass of Jews is essential. If the Jewish population remains stable at its current five million plus while the U.S. population continues to grow, the Jewish population is an ever-decreasing proportion of the total. For many years, Judaism has been the third religion in the United States, part of the familiar Protestant-Catholic-Jewish trilogy, even though Jews constitute a minute proportion of the total. But the number of Muslims in the United States has now equaled or perhaps even surpassed the number of Jews, owing to immigration and conversion, especially among the Black community. Asian religions, especially Buddhism, also continue to grow through immigration and conversion. Other religions are likely to emerge as well.

Growing the number of Jews is necessary and desirable for several reasons. First, Jews exert substantial political influence because of their heavy voting patterns and their location in key states having large electoral voting blocs, such as New York, California,

Florida, Illinois, Pennsylvania, New Jersey, and Ohio. The degree of influence depends on whether there are one million or two million voters, more or less. The size of the Jewish population matters a great deal in the political arena in terms of support for Israel as well. Issues such as legislation concerned with protection of religious minorities, separation of church and state, and guarantees of religious freedom, are of great concern to Jews. A strong political voice is crucial in helping to maintain Jewish interests.

Adequate numbers are also necessary to maintain the organizational and institutional network that reinforces Jewish community and identity. This includes Jewish community centers, Jewish newspapers, human service networks for the elderly, Jewish education systems, and so on. These services help define the community. Indeed, they constitute essential elements of the community. Without enough students or financial support, schools can collapse. Newspapers require enough circulation to make them viable. The fabric of the Jewish community is woven through its organizational and institutional network, which in turn is supported by membership dues, fees for service, and philanthropic contributions. Much of this network can disintegrate without adequate numbers to sustain it. Communities age and disperse. Jews and others have seen their communities decline and virtually disappear in cities and towns throughout North America, especially in the Midwest and South, once the critical mass of Jews was no longer present to sustain a synagogue, for example. Even without disappearance, it is conceivable that many communities could lose their vibrancy as they become unable to sustain innovative and creative life because the numbers have declined.

Perceptions of stability and growth or decline can lead to self-fulfilling prophecies, in either direction. A community that is seen to be vibrant, attracting members, retaining its own, and flourishing is likely to retain its members and attract others. On the other hand, a community that is aging without replacing its numbers and unable to attract people from outside is likely to fulfill the image of being in decline. Communities that believe they are in decline abandon institutions, cut services, and plan for a more limited future, which in turn is defined through limited vision of what might be. Communities that plan for growth often achieve the goal by promoting it.

Sometimes platitudes, old wives' tales, and conventional wisdom have important strategic purpose and meaning. Certainly, one of the oldest and most accepted platitudes is that there is strength in numbers; more Jews is better than fewer Jews, all things being equal. Of course, it would be better to have five million highly committed Jews than ten million marginally committed Jews. But this is a specious argument. It would be better to have ten million highly committed Jews than five-and-a-half million. The Jewish community need not strive for higher numbers at the expense of more committed, more observant, more highly identified, and more participatory Jews. The goal is to achieve both.

Arguments about whether or not the Jewish community should concentrate on strengthening the core of committed Jews or instead reach out to marginal Jewish populations misses the point altogether. Such arguments assume that there are only two strategies for strengthening the Jewish community and that they are both internal to the current population of American Jews. How about the vast possibilities outside our gates?

The growth in numbers that comes by making stronger institutions also gives Jews greater political power—the ability to be influential. Power and influence are meaningless for their own sake. However, power and influence can be used to affect the world positively, to fulfill the mission of Judaism, to carry out its role to be a light unto the nations. Imagine a larger and more committed, more enthusiastic Jewish population even more dedicated to the performance of *mitzvot*, dedicated to social justice and the mission to repair an increasingly broken world.

8

What We Do That Works

Despite the many barriers to conversion, things are not entirely
bleak. Some people *have* knocked and found the gates un-
locked; indeed, there are more than two hundred thousand Jews-
by-choice in America today. In crucial areas, denominational policy
is changing, and some rabbis and synagogues are developing programs and procedures that encourage non-Jews to become Jewish.

Not all programs exist solely within defined denominational
walls, either. There are a small number of independent institutions
doing good work to provide information on conversion, educate
potential converts, and support new Jews-by-choice during and after
the process. These grassroots organizations may have originated
within denominations thanks to the programming of a specific
rabbi, but some have developed independently of the denominations and constitute new and separate institutions.

A sign of the increasing profile of conversion in the Jewish community is the attention that the issue is starting to receive in the
press, both secular and Jewish. What may have begun as an adjunct
response to a perceived intermarriage crisis is beginning to take on
importance in its own right. From the *New York Times* and the *San
Francisco Examiner* to the *Jerusalem Report* and the *Forward*, edi-
torials and articles have been reporting on the efforts of certain
institutions and individuals to bring more non-Jews into the Jewish community. Even our vocabulary is beginning to change a bit:

official publications and some individuals now use the term *Jew-by-choice* routinely, as the community adjusts to the idea that Jews not only allow but indeed welcome converts.

Thousands of individual acts also take place every day to help promote conversion on a small-scale basis. A potential convert may seek training from a congregational rabbi. Someone who is married to a Jew may begin to attend Shabbat services and start the path of learning. Introduction to Judaism classes exist in synagogues throughout the United States, as well as in some Jewish community centers, bureaus of Jewish education, and universities. Opportunities to learn about Judaism at a beginning level are available in many places, and those who are interested are venturing through these formal gateways to Judaism.

Policy Gates

The Orthodox Gate: Open for Some

The Orthodox movement's policy and standards for conversion are not likely to change, no matter what occurs to the demographics of the rest of the American Jewish community. For some non-Jews, this strict and traditional policy is the right policy. Some non-Jews approach Judaism after a long search for structure in their spiritual lives and in their community. The Orthodox movement provides both. For some, barriers that are easily overcome have little value, and a *Halachic* Orthodox conversion feels more genuine, more Jewish. For example, Jonathan has been exploring every denomination, trying to find a fit as he makes his way into the Jewish community. The difficulty of the Orthodox standards resonates for him: "So far, I think the real way is the hard one. I get scared by things that get too easy, something might be fishy about easy ways" (World Wide Web posting [www.havienu.org], July 17, 1998).

Once a potential convert gets past all the barriers—long and intensive studies with a rabbi, circumcision (for men), immersion in a ritual bath, appearance before a rabbinic court, and more—the person becomes a member of a supportive and often nurturing community. The gates open for a moment to allow the convert in, and then they shut tightly again behind the new Jew.

Natalie and her husband, Jim, first converted with a Reform rabbi but "didn't feel like part of the Jewish community for two main reasons: I knew I wasn't *Halachically* Jewish, and even though I didn't know exactly what a *Halachic* conversion entailed, I had a feeling I wasn't 'really' Jewish. I didn't have a very warm reception at the Reform temple where I converted because it was huge and kind of impersonal." After her conversion, she and Jim attended their Reform congregation with decreasing frequency, until they finally decided to seek an Orthodox *shul*: "The reception we had there was unbelievable. We made many friends, and even though they did not encourage us to convert—as a matter of fact, they kept asking us if we were crazy—they welcomed us into their homes for Shabbos and holidays and answered whatever questions we had. We learned with the rabbi and the cantor on a regular basis, and converted and had our second wedding in May."

For Natalie and Jim, as well as for some others who make it past the barriers, Orthodox Judaism is the most direct and unambiguous way to embrace their new identities.

The Conservative Gate

The Conservative movement has a strong policy around conversion: in accordance with Jewish law, sincere converts should be welcomed into the community. The Conservative movement also has a strong policy around intermarriage: intermarriage should be prevented. The contradictions in these policies reflect the discontinuous forces at work in the Conservative movement itself. Some rabbis focus their efforts on preventing intermarriage, a few on welcoming converts into their congregations. It is difficult, however, to follow both paths at the same time.

The choices that rabbis (and congregations) must make as to which path—prevention or promotion of conversion—to take reflect the choices a convert to Conservative Judaism must make in living a Jewish life. Conservative standards veer toward *Halacha,* and many rabbis encourage proselytes to keep kosher, observe the Sabbath according to Jewish law, and follow other tenets of traditional Jewish living. Yet, unlike converts to Orthodox Judaism, those who choose to become Conservative can pick and choose which, if any, elements of *Halacha* they would like to follow. "Enforcement" is much more random. For some people new to Judaism, this array of options is confusing: which way is the real Jewish way? For others, however, understanding the breadth of their choices and then selecting from those options makes sense. For them, the Conservative movement's contradictions are not contradictions at all, but good policy.

The Reform Gate

For the Reform movement, outreach to non-Jews, individuals seeking conversion, and interfaith couples is institutional policy. This is not to say that every Reform congregation actively engages in outreach or even holds Introduction to Judaism classes (about 80 percent do). At an institutional level, however, the entire Reform movement—the synagogue association, the rabbinic association, the seminary—is behind the effort to reach out to non-Jews.

Unlike other national synagogue associations, the UAHC has an outreach department, the focus of which is to welcome new Jews, interfaith families, and religious seekers of all faiths into the Jewish community. (The Orthodox movement has the National Jewish Outreach Program to reenergize unaffiliated Jews, and the Conservative movement supports *keruv,* encouraging mixed-married families to maintain their Jewish ties.) Initiated by Rabbi Alexander Schindler in 1978, the joint UAHC/CCAR (Central Conference of American Rabbis) Commission on Reform Jewish Outreach was created in 1983 with a "mandate to develop programming, resources, and materials for the various Outreach populations" (What Is Reform Jewish Outreach, 1997).

Initial efforts identified the needs of mixed-married couples and their children. The intention was to educate those families and find ways to help them feel comfortable and welcome within the Jewish community. This is still a large and important part of Reform outreach, and the results, according to Dru Greenwood, director of the UAHC outreach department, have been positive: "What we find is that when people learn about what Judaism is and take part in a Jewish community, they assimilate into the Jewish community, and the correlate of that is the conversion of the non-Jewish parent (sometimes when the child becomes bar or bat mitzvah). We talk all the time about how Jews are assimilating into America, but there is also assimilation into the Jewish community. Aggressive prevention doesn't work and only makes intermarrieds feel shame in the Jewish community."

The other growing area of outreach in the Reform movement is encouragement and support of programs that help non-Jews, married or single, become Jewish. The outreach department does try to get the word out that Judaism welcomes new Jews-by-choice. "A Taste of Judaism: Are You Curious?" is a free three-session course to introduce newcomers to Jewish values and thought. The course is widely advertised in mainstream secular media. The curriculum and financial support come from the UAHC, and individual rabbis and congregations publicize and deliver the course in their local communities. As of spring 1998, more than twelve thousand people—Jews and non-Jews—have attended, and about 14 percent of the non-Jews have gone on to begin the conversion process through a more comprehensive Introduction to Judaism course.

With the success of "A Taste of Judaism," more people have been seeking conversion than before. It has become apparent to the outreach department and the CCAR that potential Jews might not receive the kind of personal attention necessary to help them through the emotional turmoil of converting. In response, the department, in cooperation with the CCAR and the Hebrew Union College–Jewish Institute of Religion (HUC-JIR), has initiated an

Outreach Fellows program to "certify laypeople to work in partnership with rabbis counseling small groups of prospective Jews on such issues as authenticity, acculturation, and family concerns" (Commission on Reform Jewish Outreach, n.d. [b]).

According to Greenwood, "One impetus for creating the Outreach Fellows program is to give rabbis some help with the large numbers of people seeking conversion (several rabbis reported more than twenty at a time). They were starting to have to turn people away." The Reform movement is seeking to solve this problem by giving interested members of the community thoughtful and serious training on the history, process, and psychosocial aspects of converting so that new members of the community feel that they have a real place inside the gates. Greenwood explains: "Welcoming Jews by choice is an art and should be broadly shared. It's not something that should be a one-two-three process."

Structural Gates

Individual rabbis and individual congregations have done more to open the gates than has any official policy. There are a few fine examples of rabbis and congregations that have implemented their own programs and initiatives to welcome non-Jews into the community and invite them to become Jewish. Although some Orthodox rabbis would be willing to speak with an interested non-Jew about conversion, the majority of these innovative programmatic efforts occur in Reform and Conservative congregations, as well as in some independent institutions outside of denominational lines.

Shabbat Buddies and Other Welcoming Signs

The majority of Reform and Conservative synagogues unofficially recognize in one way or another that non-Jews attend services, often alongside a Jewish spouse or other family member. Sometimes, however, a potential convert attends alone to begin to learn about Judaism. He or she may be there as part of an introduction to

Judaism course, or as a first brave step in exploring Judaism. Accompanied by family or not, many of these non-Jews sit in the synagogue without understanding the norms, rituals, or meaning of the service (let alone the language, when the congregation recites Hebrew prayers). Left alone, they may feel unwelcome, confused, or at best simply mystified.

Some congregations have implemented welcoming programs at services that integrate the concept of outreach more fully into the synagogue. The purpose of these programs is to make sure that everyone who walks through the door feels welcome and can find the service at least intelligible, if not personally meaningful. The programs take different forms. Some congregations have volunteer ushers who act as greeters, simply welcoming all. Other programs train their ushers to recognize unfamiliar faces and ask if they would like some assistance in following the service.

Such a program made a difference to Lucy, a Filipino American woman who was nervous about attending her first service because she feared "I would be the only person of color there. The greeter was friendly and helped me locate a Shabbat buddy, a young Israeli woman about my age. I sat with [her] through the service. [She] was warm, open, and friendly." Two months later, Lucy received an invitation to meet with the membership committee and other prospective members of the congregation for a roundtable discussion about affiliating. She decided to join the synagogue, and "several weeks later the chair of the membership committee called to discuss any questions I had about joining the congregation and my decision to convert."

Follow-up calls, letters, or invitations from membership committees, synagogue boards, or other social structures within the congregation are essential components of a program to build membership. Congregations that view everyone who walks through the door— unaffiliated Jew or non-Jew—as a potential member are more likely to create welcoming and warm experiences for prospective converts. The program need not even be formal; a greeting at the door from an usher or other member of the congregation may be enough to make the interested stranger decide to return.

Getting the (Electronic) Word Out

One of the more daunting barriers to promoting proactive conversion is simply getting the message out that Judaism welcomes converts. Some synagogues and other institutions are moving beyond their reticence to announcing their presence. Some rabbis are willing to say out loud and in public, "We welcome you. Come explore Judaism."

The Internet has become a growing resource for those wanting to disseminate information and for those seeking it. Discussion groups, e-mail listservs (distribution centers for e-mail correspondence around a particular subject), chat rooms, frequently-asked-question (FAQ) pages, and other online resources are vital information centers for those who might not otherwise consider Judaism. Many synagogues have their own Web pages, with general information about Judaism, Jewish holidays, and Jewish tradition, as well as specific data about the congregation.

The central online information resource about conversion is the aptly named Conversion to Judaism home page (www.convert.org). Created by Lawrence J. Epstein as part of the Conversion to Judaism Resource Center (a project of the Suffolk County, New York, Jewish Communal Planning Council), the Conversion to Judaism home page receives visits from at least a hundred people every day. Visitors come to the site to find information, local resources, rabbis, and general support for the process of becoming a Jew. According to the Resource Center's executive director, Susan Lustig, the home page has "been a very significant way for people to get information in a confidential way. They can then pursue their own path. We don't provide classes; we provide a welcome for people who want to explore the possibility of becoming Jewish. We have rabbis of every ilk on our board of directors. We have sent our brochures to every state in the Union and approximately twenty countries, from Scandinavia and South Africa to the Philippines."

The Conversion to Judaism Resource Center also provides free brochures and pamphlets on how to discuss conversion with family and friends, making the decision to convert, and offering a Conversion to Judaism class. The same brochures are reproduced online. The center's accessibility and its nondenominational, nonthreatening, and proactive stance on conversion have opened the minds of many non-Jews who might not otherwise have considered it possible to become Jewish. According to Epstein, some of the people he has spoken with at first "don't think they are worthy enough to be Jewish because Judaism is such an 'elevated system.' Jews are so close to God as the chosen people that they don't believe themselves worthy of being Jewish, of being part of that elite." The Resource Center helps them move past their fears and begin to gather the information necessary to see Judaism as a viable option.

The anonymity and boundlessness of the Internet allow seekers of information about Judaism to explore privately and without commitment before they determine they are ready. Communities of converts and proselytes are growing online through e-mail exchanges and message boards, where Jews-by-choice offer advice to those who are thinking about conversion and support to those who have already completed the process and are finding their way into the community. These cybercommunities fill a void left by the absence of such support in local communities, and the number and quality of these resources is growing quickly.

The institutional world has taken notice. In addition to the synagogue Web sites, each denomination now maintains a place in cyberspace, and federations are becoming players. As part of their Jewish continuity grant program, UJA–Federation of New York has provided funding for the Hillel Institute (Queens and Nassau and Suffolk counties, New York) to put up a Web site and offer a twenty-four-week Introduction to Judaism course for those interested in converting under the auspices of the Conservative movement. The Jewish Outreach Institute (a resource for interfaith families sponsored by City University of New York) hosts a message board on conversion, and many Jews-by-choice have created their own Web sites to tell their stories and urge others to explore Judaism.

Announcing . . . Judaism

Public announcements of Introduction to Judaism and other classes— open to Jews and non-Jews alike—are appearing in secular papers in increasing numbers and to increasing audiences. The nature of these announcements still varies greatly, with some of them diffident and apologetic for suggesting that Judaism might be of interest to non-Jews. Others, however, are beginning to demonstrate the confidence that correlates with the success of the Jewish community in America. The strongest of the announcements include an unambiguous message that non-Jews as well as Jews are invited to learn more about Judaism. For example, the ad for an Introduction to Judaism course offered by congregation Schaarai Zedek, a Reform congregation in Tampa, begins with the headline: "Judaism is 4,000 years old. Rabbi Birnholz's Introductory Course Takes 8 Weeks." It specifies that the course is "ideal for non-Jews, Jews by Birth, Jews by Choice, Intermarried Couples, and Unaffiliated Jews." The announcement does not mention conversion, and it is inviting, personal, and straightforward: "If this informative course sounds like it's right for you or someone you love, call. . . ." Others contain similarly welcoming language. United Synagogue in Hoboken, New Jersey, specifies that its Introduction to Judaism class is "for Jews and non-Jews who seek a deeper understanding of Judaism." Temple Akiba in Culver City, California, asks, "Is Judaism for Non-Jews?" and answers its own question: "Maybe: Sample Jewish spirituality through study and worship." These models need to be replicated and expanded in every community that offers an Introduction to Judaism class.

Foundations

Some of the funding for these announcements is coming from another important segment of the nondenominational institutional world: private foundations. The National Center to Encourage Judaism (NCEJ) is a private, nonprofit family foundation whose sole purpose, according to founder Ash Gerecht, is to award "grants to synagogues or consortia that conduct adult Judaism classes inviting everyone to attend." The grants provide up to one-half the cost of placing announcements for the classes in the secular press. The announcements must specify that the class is open to non-Jews as well as Jews. The NCEJ also awards bonus grants to synagogues with programs "[(1)] actively welcoming attendees at oneg shabbats and kiddush . . . , (2) further integrating interfaith couples and families and new converts into Judaism with specific, supportive classes, holding preparations sessions, etc., [and] (3) having available and providing free various pamphlets and booklets on conversion to Judaism" (Gerecht, 1998, p. 7).

The NCEJ is a fine model of the kind of support that foundations can provide without having to initiate programs of their own. NCEJ grants encourage institutions to increase the visibility of their own programs and improve the quality of their publicity. Through its quarterly newsletter, the *Jewish Proclaimer*, which contains samples of successful announcements and reports of turnout from classes around the country, the NCEJ creates a de facto network of institutions with a shared goal. The large denominational structures are beginning to respond: the UAHC helps distribute grant applications to its member congregations to encourage them to publicize their own classes.

Educational Models

At the heart of all the good work now beginning to occur that promotes conversion in the Jewish community are the classes and workshops meant to introduce the proselyte to Judaism. Most synagogues in America offer their own classes, create joint courses with other congregations of the same denomination, or direct prospective converts to a Jewish community center or other community organization that offers adult learning. Classes are generally low-cost, and in many cases even the small fee can be waived if necessary. Some congregations make a gift of the books used in class, a welcoming and generous introduction to the synagogue. These are good and positive developments.

A few programs around the country stand out as models of accessible, high-quality educational experiences. They tend to be older, more established programs, with more than one educator or rabbi teaching the course. They often provide perspectives and experiences from all denominations of Judaism so that prospective converts can make choices about which branch of Judaism best serves them. They attract large numbers of people every year and have become some of the more important gate-openers in the Jewish community. Three such programs serve as good examples: one in a synagogue, one at a university, and one outside the formal institutional structure.

Valley Beth Sholom

The Keruv Center of Valley Beth Sholom, a large Conservative congregation in Encino, California, offers a comprehensive program of education and support for anyone wanting to come closer to Judaism. At the forefront of Valley Beth Sholom's efforts is Rabbi Harold Schulweis, a respected and influential thinker and one of the vocal supporters of proactive conversion in the Jewish community. In an article in Forward, Schulweis explains the impetus behind the creation of the Keruv Center when he asks: "What is the purpose of Judaism if not to share its wisdom, ethics, and spirituality to the world?" (Kessler, 1998, p. 1).

Unlike the UAHC institutional approach to outreach, the Conservative movement does not have a formal program to seek converts. Valley Beth Sholom's Keruv Center program should serve as a model for the denomination, because, like the Conservative movement itself, it offers choices to participants. The announcement for the 1998 classes sets the welcoming tone for the course: "Beyond Bagels!" proclaims the headline. "An Introduction to Judaism: A Pluralistic Outreach." The announcement explains that the thirteen-week course is "for Jews seeking a deeper connection, for non-Jews searching for a tradition of wisdom, faith, and meaning. Presented by the best of Orthodox, Conservative, Reform, and Reconstructionist rabbis. Open to the public—No charge!"

The course is pluralistic because rabbis of all denominations, both congregational and noncongregational, offer lectures, opinions, and ideas to participants. At the end of the course, those non-Jews interested in conversion can choose which denomination they would like to join, and the Keruv Center directs them to an appropriate rabbi to continue the process.

In addition to its public announcements, the Keruv Center publicizes its work through an informative brochure available from the congregation and throughout the San Fernando Valley. The 1997–98 brochure "extends an invitation to learn, experience, and come close to the centuries-old wisdom of Judaism" to "unaffiliated Jews, disaffected and alienated from their history and traditions, who see a way home to a Judaism that is accepting, wise, morally powerful, and intellectually alive" and to "'unchurched' Christians who would welcome an invitation to an authentic, deep, inspiring and warm spirituality—a spirituality that appreciates questions, embraces complexity, and affirms life." The brochure is intelligent, challenging, and confident—everything the Jewish community can be to its members. It takes an unapologetically proactive stance toward inviting "'unchurched' Christians" to explore Judaism. As a good marketing piece should, it touts the benefits of Judaism without denigrating the competition.

The Keruv Center has also initiated a mentoring program for Valley Beth Sholom members. A model of strong, positive policy and structure, the mentoring program is similar to the UAHC Outreach Fellows program. It prepares members of the congregation to share their experiences with prospective converts and help them through the process of becoming a Jew. It formalizes what should be a standard component of every congregation in the United States and increases congregation members' awareness of the unique and sometimes difficult journey of choosing to become a Jew.

The Miller Introduction to Judaism Program

The Miller Introduction to Judaism Program of the Zeigler School of Rabbinics at the University of Judaism in Los Angeles is offered monthly, every day of the week except Friday and Saturday. Rabbi Neal Weinberg, the director of the program, emphasizes the flexible nature of the program: "If you miss one class, you can make it up another day in a subsequent month. We even have satellite classes in local synagogues for people who live too far from the university." This flexibility takes into account the reality of the lives that many prospective converts lead: children, jobs, and other outside demands make it difficult to attend an evening class with regularity.

Like other model programs, the Miller program introduces students to Judaism through lecture, holiday celebrations, and experiential learning. More academically rigorous than most programs, each class session lasts three-and-a-half hours with "one ten-minute prayer aerobic session" at the beginning and during period breaks. In addition, students participate in a twenty-four-hour *Shabbaton*, or retreat, at a local synagogue. The purpose of the retreat is to experience as a member of a synagogue the celebration of the Sabbath as well as some of the more social aspects of being Jewish, such as Israeli folk dancing and kosher meals.

The program also requires that prospective converts participate in support groups conducted by a marriage and family therapist and a coordinator, who is also a Jew by choice. Like other exemplars, Weinberg does not think that conversion is solely a religious process: "I don't think it's enough to study Judaism alone. I find that almost none of the other programs have support groups. There is also a need for dealing with the emotional and psychological aspects of Judaism." Support group meetings cover specific themes, including family dynamics, holiday lifestyle conflicts, and developing a Jewish identity. Associated with the support groups is fulfillment of certain experiential requirements such as visiting a kosher market or bakery, reading a book with a Jewish theme, or attending a Jewish cultural event.

Because the University of Judaism is not a congregation, it can, according to Weinberg, offer a more neutral and personalized approach to learning about Judaism. Although associated with the Conservative movement, Weinberg takes "a pluralistic approach that teaches about all the movements in Judaism."

The Center for Conversion to Judaism

Founded by Rabbi Stephen C. Lerner in 1981, the Center for Conversion to Judaism is an independent (noncongregational) institute affiliated with the Conservative movement. Based in northern New Jersey, it also has offices in Manhattan, Westchester County (New York), and Chicago. The purpose of the center, according to its brochure, is "to introduce both Jews and non-Jews to Jewish learning and living." The center is solely an educational institution and does not perform conversions. Instead, it helps proselytes find a sponsoring rabbi in their own communities and then acts as a mentor for candidates through the process. Both the noncongregational nature of the center as well as its emphasis on a combination of study *and* experience make the program worthy of replication.

Study is rigorous (twenty-five to thirty sessions over nine months), and standards are high. Participants are expected to attend Shabbat services at least three times a month and to follow the laws of *kashrut*. (Proselytes have choices within even these rigorous standards.) At the same time, the syllabus for the course provides for independent exploration and flexibility: "The goal is to climb a ladder of Jewish observance, faith and commitment. Since the ladder stretches toward heaven, we recognize that no two people will reach the same rung"

(Lerner, n.d.). To help students with their climb, the center's rabbis and rabbinic students guide potential converts through formal classes, religious services, weekend retreats, holiday workshops, and other experiences meant to provide a taste of the full range of Jewish life.

Whereas many rabbis consider marriage to a Jew insufficient reason to convert, Lerner's belief is that purely religious conversion is not enough to build a strong Jewish community. "If we want to forget about Jewish peoplehood, we can convert them and forget about it. Better to convert *with* someone, for community, for sharing, than to do so for the classically emphasized view, which is for its own sake." To that end, the Center for Conversion to Judaism requires that all proselytes and their partners join a support group. Like the UAHC Outreach Fellows and the Keruv Center's mentors, these support groups help participants understand the conflicted feelings they may have about giving up their past religious identity, as well as the challenges they may face inside the Jewish community as Jews-by-choice.

When the Gates Are Open

Any congregation can provide a model of good programming, sensitive social structures, and welcoming administrations. Any rabbi can be an official exemplar of openness and support. In the end, it is most often the behavior, attitude, and tone of the individual representatives of Judaism—official or unofficial, in the aisles of the synagogue or on the streets—that have the most power to make the gates appear open or closed to a prospective Jew.

The best models make use of everyday words and deeds: the receptionist who with genuine enthusiasm and warmth answers questions from a stranger, the person who moves over to sit next to the nervous outsider on a Friday evening and explain what is happening during services, the rabbi who offers High Holiday tickets to the non-Jew calling to ask about conversion a day before Rosh Hashanah. In innumerable ways, Jews of all denominations are beginning to open up, not just to the *idea* of welcoming Jews-by-choice into our community, but to the new Jews themselves, who have made a brave and bold choice to knock on the gates and ask to come inside.

The Need to Replicate

Successful prototypical programs for proactive conversion dot the landscape. This chapter examines a few of those programs as models of successful policy, structure, and procedure. It is by no means an exhaustive survey of all the positive steps being taken in the Jewish community today regarding proactive conversion. Other rabbis and other synagogues are doing good work. For example, Patti Moskovitz, a Jewish educator in northern California, offers tutoring and guidance for those wishing to convert or to learn more about their own Jewish heritage. Her students come to her through rabbinic referral. Her goal is simple and exemplary: "to transmit Judaism to everyone who studies with me in as pure and loving a manner as I possibly can." There should be more such offerings.

It is important to pay attention to what is developing. We need to create networks of like-minded individuals and institutions to avoid reinventing classes, seminars, support groups, and written materials for potential and actual Jews-by-choice. Expanding the best programs within the communities where they already exist and exporting them to other communities would accomplish a great deal.

9

How to Open the Gates

The stage is set for proactive conversion.

We are unmistakably in a period of remarkable transition, facing the opportunity to achieve integration without dissolution. The United States nurtures Jewish distinctiveness. Dual-identity groups have become not only more acceptable but desirable: African Americans, Asian Americans, Italian Americans, and, of course, Jewish Americans. If we Jews abandon our identity in the United States today, it is not because we are forced to do so to be part of American society. Religious adherence is so valued in the United States that Jews are considered to be *more* American, *better* Americans, by being *more* Jewish, not less. It is incomprehensible to many Jews that being more visible and articulate Jews actually improves our acceptability to a predominantly Christian society.

Even though the purpose and meaning of being Jewish needs to be reaffirmed, most Jews retain their Jewish identity and are still engaged in some Jewish behaviors. Jewish identity does not translate often into the most traditional religious behaviors, such as keeping kosher, but it does express itself in a number of ways that bear some discussion.

Havurot, expanded observance of Jewish rituals, and other dimensions of spiritual and religious life are attracting significant proportions of younger Jews. Jewish leadership has become more interested in Jewish learning and tradition, and aspects of traditional Judaism are becoming part of everyday life, even as new forms of Judaism are developing and being expressed.

Most Jews still attend synagogue on the High Holiday days, and most participate in a Passover Seder. Most receive some Jewish education. Some of the third and fourth generations and beyond are more observant and involved than previous generations. Younger generations *choose* involvement in Jewish life, while previous generations participated partly as a function of external pressure as well as ethnic isolation.

The active participation of younger Jews is remarkable. They have kept Judaism alive far beyond the first and second areas of settlement in the cities and suburbs and have transplanted an ethnoreligious culture into geographical dispersion, within metropolitan areas and across the new Jewish communities emerging throughout the United States. It is a testament to the possibilities for even greater vitality in the future that Jews have maintained high levels of in-group cohesion and religious revival, in spite of the contextual obstacles.

Judaism provides familiarity, comfort, and stability. It provides the continuity of a set of ideas, a people, and ways of life. Judaism in the United States continues to incorporate American ideas and practices into traditional Judaism, just as Jewish culture continues to influence the general American society. We have engaged in this borrowing and blending before. Redefining belief and practice through absorbing host cultures in Jewish ways makes us grow. Rethinking conversion is part of the next redefinition process.

Strategies for Inclusion

The Jewish community needs to offer support programs for mixed-married couples and their children. Navigating the landscape of mixed religious identities can be extremely difficult. The Jewish community cannot be punitive just because a Jew makes a choice to marry somebody who is not Jewish. Individuals make this choice for all kinds of reasons. Some Jews marry non-Jews because of their indifference or hostility to Judaism. However, most simply fall in love with somebody who is not Jewish, a matter of odds in an integrated society. The Jewish community needs to be more sympathetic and supportive to those who are in a mixed marriage. Calls to focus on the "core," with limited expenditures for mixed-married couples, come partly from disappointment and anger: we feel cheated. The community should offer a vast array of support programs in terms of counseling, workshops, educational forums, Seders for mixed-married couples, and so on. Mixed-married couples do not require tough love. Mixed-marrieds should not be ignored by the Jewish community while we concentrate on the core: the good Jews, the salvageable Jews.

Some proportion of Jews who continue to live with non-Jews will not be candidates for conversion. The institutional structure must be able to accommodate what will be a large and growing number of families of mixed parentage and identity. Community centers, synagogue, day camps, overnight camps, and every other Jewish organization and institution must deal with the reality of the mixed-married population. Currently, the Jewish community has little structure to deal with this population. Expenditures are minuscule and the approaches are confused. Some couples need counseling and therapy, some need advice, and some need direction. Others just need to be left alone.

Specifically dealing with mixed marriage is very different from determining how to approach conversion. Programs for mixed-married couples may lead to conversion and creation of Jewish homes. But overall communal strategies must also recognize that conversion and being Jewish are not for everyone. Still, mixed-married households are to remain part of the Jewish community in some way. Therefore, programs or approaches to mixed marriage cannot be conceived of as solving the "intermarriage problem," or even oriented toward making everybody Jews.

Programs for mixed marrieds are a place for understanding, compassion, and tolerance. Communal strategies for growth and for creating more Jews must be distinct from strategies and programs in dealing with the mixed-married population. If Jews become less hysterical about mixed marrieds representing the destruction of Judaism, then mixed marrieds can be approached differently—not as the carriers of Jewish doom, a disease to be cured, a battle to be won, a holocaust to be avoided. The Jewish community is compassionate only when it feels safe enough to show compassion. This happens only if we grow enough by making more households Jewish through converts joining our ranks.

A second set of programs for inclusion should be developed for those who actively seek Judaism. Individuals may inquire about Jewish life because they have read a Jewish book, seen a Jewish film, or come into contact with Jewish individuals. For whatever reason, non-Jews come knocking on one door or another of the Jewish community seeking information, encouragement, or understanding. A good communal strategy of proactive conversion would find as many non-Jews attracted to Judaism who are *not* married to Jews, if not more. They come because they are attracted to Judaism, not to a specific Jew. The Jewish community needs an institutional and programmatic system to be available to those who come seeking. The current approach is one of skepticism, and more often than not there is no door on which to knock. The communal resources committed to having Jewish life accessible to non-Jews is practically nonexistent. Indeed, easily accessible, highly visible avenues into the Jewish community are often difficult to find, even for those who are born Jewish.

Maintaining Standards

Every culture has rites of initiation and passage. The act of conversion should require no less. The actual conversion is different from the process of transformation. It occurs in different ways, with different rules, depending on the individual or denomination. Since the rites of passage really are both religious and cultural, the community must differentiate between the paths to conversion and the ritual of conversion.

At the point of actual conversion, what should be required of someone to declare himself or herself part of the Jewish people? First, the ritual for conversion must be simple. This requires *mikvah* and circumcision for a male, and the circumcision can be symbolic. At the same time, someone who commits to the Jewish people must make two pledges: to instruct the children in Jewish life, and not to raise a child in another religion. This must be coupled with the person's own commitment not to practice another religion and accept the essence of ethical monotheism.

Target Groups for Inclusion

America is a marketplace of religions where people switch their religious identities often and should feel free to do so. If a faith tradition has beauty, meaning, and fulfillment associated with it, it seems logical that a religious group would want to share these benefits with others.

Judaism should be offered to any individual who feels a deep spiritual commitment to God or worship or the desire to be part of the Jewish people. Such efforts should not be invasive or disrespectful. No religion should attempt to recruit individuals from another religion by degrading or criticizing some other faith tradition. Southern Baptists, for example, should not approach Jews because they are "incomplete," "destined for hell," or "practicing an inferior religion." No religious group should use coercive efforts, strong-arm tactics, threats, or snide and despairing techniques to entice someone into another faith tradition. However, if Southern Baptists approach Jews to spread the joy of worshiping Christ and the meaning and purpose that comes from accepting Christ, then they should be free to do so. In the same way, Jews should be free to approach members of other religious groups, including Southern Baptists, to advocate for the joys of Jewish peoplehood, the theology of Judaism, the richness of ritual practice, and the benefits of being part of the Jewish tradition. It could well be that more Southern Baptists would become Jews, as opposed to the other way around.

Lawrence Epstein (1994) summarizes from the literature the reasons that individuals may elect to become Jews. He classifies them as spiritual, romantic, communal, and personal. Different reasons apply to different groups targeted for inclusion. As we devise strategies for inclusion, we have to be mindful of these myriad reasons and how they apply to different individuals and groups. Here is his list.

Spiritual Reasons

1. Judaism was seen to provide a religious world view, or a set of values, or an ethic that was better than the religion or world view previously held.
2. Judaism was considered important because Jesus was a Jew.
3. God was providing direction in some way to come to Judaism.
4. Judaism simply was coherent with common sense about what religion should be.
5. Jewish religious services were attractive.
6. Judaism's practices were very realistic.
7. Judaism provided good role models for a needed spiritual identity through biblical figures as well as contemporaries such as a romantic partner, friend, doctor, or employer.
8. There was a deep-seated sense of a religious void, and Judaism filled that void.
9. A specific personal event, such as a death, a divorce, or the breakup of a relationship, precipitated a religious crisis that resulted in a need to find a new religious self-definition.

Romantic Reasons

1. It was desired that the children in a marriage have a Jewish identity.
2. There was a wish to be married in a Jewish ceremony.

3. There was a concern that children be raised in a unified spiritual home.
4. There was a desire to avoid inevitable fights over such questions as theology and religious observance.
5. There was a wish to please the in-laws.
6. The Jewish romantic partner would be pleased.
7. Conversion provided a opportunity to share the romantic partner's religion and thus bring the couple closer together.

Communal Reasons

1. Jews were admired for their survival in the face of adversity.
2. Jews were seen as forming a warm community, and it was seen as desirous to join such a community.
3. Judaism was seen as having a distinguished history and joining that tradition was seen as a worthy goal.
4. Jews were thought to lead better lives than Gentiles.
5. The convert had numerous Jewish friends.
6. The convert had a desire to identify with the Jewish people and become part of the fate of the Jews.
7. Jewish social life was seen as attractive.

Personal Reasons

1. There was a belief that becoming Jewish would lead to gains in such things as status.
2. The idea of joining a new religion was seen as exciting.
3. Judaism had been a "forbidden fruit," so that becoming Jewish was exciting.
4. Becoming Jewish was a way of separation from birth parents (pp. 6–8).

It is clear that motivations are quite extensive—Epstein lists twenty-seven reasons in four categories. The draws to Judaism are so plentiful that an open, positive attitude and institutional approach on the part of Jews could produce an avalanche of individuals who are interested—because they are seeking all kinds of guidance, fulfillment, community, learning, and the many rewards that Judaism has to offer.

Figure 9.1 shows the target groups for major inclusion efforts to increase the Jewish community. Group one is the non-Jewish spouses of Jews. It is a group with which the Jewish community has a maximum amount of contact and impact. Spouses have already entered the realm of Jewish life to one degree or another by living with someone who is Jewish. Over time, a significant proportion of those with no religion or those who are practicing as Jews could become part of the Jewish people. Even those practicing another religion could change their minds and hearts.

Because non-Jewish spouses exhibit tremendous differences and levels of religiosity and identity, no single set of strategies for promoting conversion is appropriate for this group. At the same time, the Jewish community has to develop multiple strategies for the Jewish partner in these relationships. The partners are often ambivalent, uncertain, fearful, or even hostile about their own Jewish identity. They may be more reluctant than the non-Jewish spouse to participate in efforts to help the spouse become a Jew. Alternatively, they may wish deeply for the spouse to be a Jew but are afraid of offending the partner by asking him or her to convert because they believe it is wrong in principle to ask anyone to convert. The Jewish community must be very careful about how it approaches non-Jewish spouses. Being overly aggressive is undoubtedly counterproductive. Enormous patience is required; the conversion process could take five, ten, fifteen years or more and in some cases still not lead to conversion. Insisting on conversion before marriage, for example, lessens the possibility of increasing the number of non-Jewish spouses who become part of the Jewish community. Most simply are not ready.

However, the community does need to be clear that it strongly prefers that spouses become Jews at some point. The message should

Figure 9.1. Target Groups for Major Inclusion Efforts

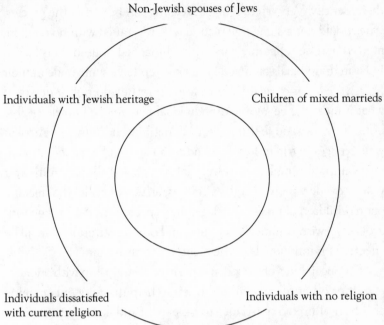

Non-Jewish spouses of Jews

Individuals with Jewish heritage

Children of mixed marrieds

Individuals dissatisfied
with current religion

Individuals with no religion

be, "We would like you to become Jewish because we would like to share our beliefs and our community with you. We believe it would be beneficial for you, your family, and the community to join and participate." This is a different message from "We will reject you if you reject us. We will condemn you if you say no; we consider you to be part of the problem, the disease of the Jewish community, if you do not convert." And we must mean what we say. We cannot be critical of those who choose not to convert.

The children of mixed marrieds are a second logical constituency to advocate for inclusion into Judaism. The Jewish community can be much more proactive in nurturing these children with programmatic initiatives at Jewish community centers, home study, volunteer programs, and a whole range of activities to involve young people.

Furthermore, a concerted effort should be instituted for those age eighteen and older. Young adults in their college, graduate school, and postgraduate school years usually are seeking to define their identity. Very often, religious seeking can be part of the process. One should not assume that a child who was raised with no religion, more than one religion, or in a mixed-married household is lost to Judaism. Individuals of mixed heritage often have some pride in their Jewish roots, or curiosity about it even if they do not understand what it means to be a Jew. An individual may not be knowledgeable but still have good feelings about being Jewish. Points of entry at younger ages (a trip to Israel, attending a Passover Seder, Jewish summer camp) can make an individual receptive to Judaism in later years. A wide variety of college courses; an active Hillel that reaches out to children of mixed marriages; and specific efforts through synagogues, Jewish community centers, and other institutions can all be effective for individuals in the eighteen-to-thirty range.

The specialness of a good and positive relationship with a grandparent or other relative may also serve the purpose of encouraging children of mixed marriages to be part of Judaism. A relative or friend who is joyful, enthusiastic, knowledgeable, and positive about his or her Judaism may have an enormous effect. A grandparent may have a more powerful effect than all of the day schools, supplemental schools, and synagogue attendance combined.

A third target group is that of individuals with Jewish heritage. There are now millions of them in the United States. Indeed, within a few years there are likely to be more people of Jewish heritage than individuals actually having two born Jewish parents. Some individuals are vaguely aware of their Jewish heritage and are intrigued by the Jewish part of their history. Sometimes they practice other religions, or they may be among the American unchurched. Because Judaism has been part of their story and of their past, some are inclined at least to think about what it means to have Jewish roots. They may have some inclination toward exploring the Jewish component of their identity. With proper nurturing, many could reclaim their Jewish past and integrate it into their current lives.

The fourth target group for Jewish inclusion is individuals with no religion. Polls consistently show that millions of Americans are unchurched. Some in this group do not believe in God or organized religion and do not want to be part of a faith tradition. Others are seeking but cannot find a faith tradition in which they feel comfortable or motivated. Some may be disengaged from the religion in which they were raised, having decided it was not for them. Others have been brought up with no religion and are seeking religious fulfillment. The thousands of self-help groups, television evangelistic successes, and pop culture fads of all kinds that promise rewarding lives and meaningful existence are testimony to the vast numbers of Americans who are longing for something purposeful in life. Judaism can be an attractive alternative for millions of these individuals who are interested in faith, community, or both.

The fifth target group consists of individuals who are practicing another religion but dissatisfied with it. Some individuals follow their current religion because they have not thought of anything else; it is simply the way they were raised. They have not actively sought alternatives even though they may be dissatisfied with the worship services, the theology, or the community their faith tradition provides.

What Are the Next Steps?

Figure 9.2 shows the steps needed to initiate the proactive conversion process in the United States.

Changing Ideology

The first step is to change the ideology. It probably takes five to ten years for new ideas to work their way into the system and for the proactive conversion agenda to take form.

Creating New Institutions

Step two is to create new institutions. The community must create a National Center for Jewish Inclusion (with the agenda of promoting

Figure 9.2. Steps to Initiate the Proactive Conversion Process

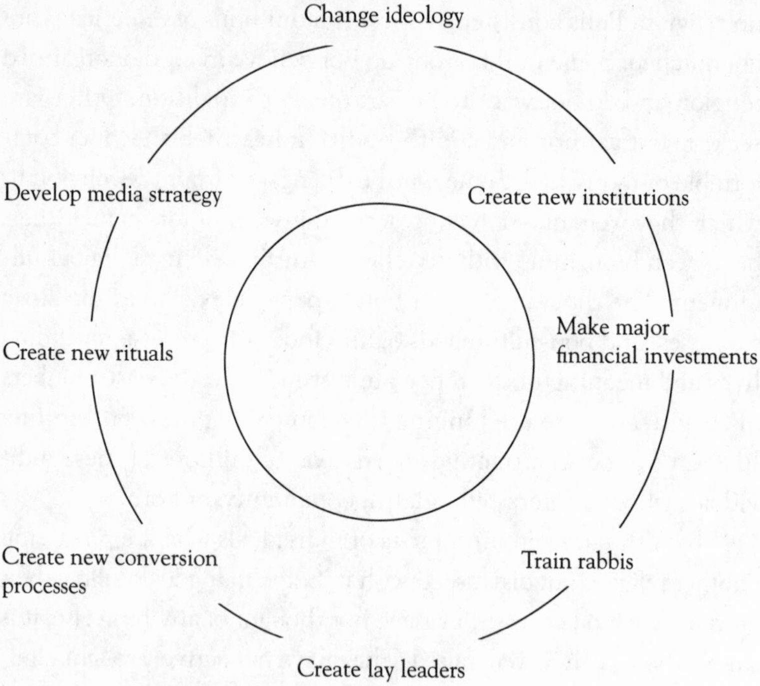

Change ideology

Develop media strategy

Create new institutions

Create new rituals

Make major
financial investments

Create new conversion
processes

Train rabbis

Create lay leaders

conversion throughout the United States) and local conversion centers as well.

Making a Major Investment

Step three is a major dollar investment. Billions of dollars have to be expended over a period of years. The Jewish community has billions in reserve, and this is a compelling application for major investment.

Training Rabbis

Step four is to create an in-service program for retraining the current rabbinate. Of the thousands of rabbis in the field, few are likely equipped at present to be open advocates for conversion; therefore, creating curricula and leadership development programs for conversion is a key part of the initiative. Rabbinic training for future rabbis needs to be restructured within the seminaries. There must be major incentive funding for the seminaries to create new curricula, to train rabbis to approach conversion positively and give them the tools to promote conversion.

Creating Lay Advocates

Step five is to create a core of advocates for Judaism, lay individuals who can recruit and teach others. They are to work in tandem with the rabbinic core to positively promote Judaism. Since the conversion process is more than just learning laws and rules, non-rabbis may be more helpful.

Creating New Rituals

Step six is to create a new set of celebrations surrounding conversion, meant to bring conversion out of the closet and make it a ceremony that rivals the bar or bat mitzvah as an entry point in Jewish life. Some individuals, of course, may choose not to do so; they prefer their conversion to be low-key. But the opportunity to have an open and celebratory declaration of Judaism should be part of the institutional structure.

Creating New Conversion Processes

Step seven is to create a new set of processes for conversion, including various tracks along time (some conversion programs can be designed for people who will take a year, for others five or twenty). Conversion programs might require up-front commitment; others can proceed by way of five-step (or ten- or twelve-step) programs in which people commit only to part one and then advance to part two or three and so on willingly. One may undertake the path of conversion at the outset without committing oneself to becoming a Jew prior to reaching understanding of what it means.

Developing New Materials

Step eight is to develop materials for use in all the media, both Jewish and non-Jewish, including TV, the Internet, and radio, to actively promote Judaism. This step comes last in that all other elements of the conversion initiative need to be in place first, in anticipation of public response.

Creating New Institutions for Conversion

The key to proactive conversion is accessibility. Individuals who want to become Jews must have a point of entry and an access route into Jewish life. To accomplish this goal, a number of critical elements are required. Information and knowledge—where do I go, who do I talk to, what do I have to do—must be easily accessed. Those who are most aggressive in breaking down the institutional doors of synagogues or other institutions to say that they are interested and want to participate may actually gain access. But information and knowledge should be shared intensively and aggressively. They should not be accessible only to those who are lucky or strong enough. Practically, this means clear and specific information on learning about Judaism needs to be available through the print media, radio and television, the Internet, and other avenues.

Information must also include an unequivocal message that these classes are open to both Jews who want to learn about their heritage and non-Jews who wish to explore Judaism. Institutions, organizations, companies, schools, or clubs that are truly interested in growing and attracting more constituents do not rely only on word-of-mouth but use available information networks to promote who they are and what they are about so as to attract users, customers, or members.

Informal communication networks are also vital. Individuals who could come into contact with potential converts need to be properly trained to interact with them. They must learn a new language, be careful to understand the sensitivities of those with whom they are speaking, be knowledgeable about what is available in terms of conversion in the synagogue or elsewhere, and be enthusiastic in transmitting this information. They themselves must be passionate Jews and communicate this passion to those interested in becoming Jews.

The same can be said for programs to train ushers at worship services, secretaries handling inquiries about High Holiday tickets, or educational administrators dealing with queries at Hebrew school. Creating warm and welcoming institutions should be a key agenda item for the Jewish community for born Jews as well as for potential converts. By thinking about how we welcome the stranger, we actually improve how we structure our organizations and institutions.

The Jewish community needs conversion programs at synagogues and institutions. We cannot assume that the current organizational and institutional structure is able to absorb the programmatic agenda of proactive conversion without new personnel and institutional support.

Institutions have existing missions, purposes, and responsibilities; most especially, synagogues are woefully understaffed. The day-to-day operations of a synagogue—making sure that the boiler is repaired, the High Holiday seats are assigned, and the *bar* or *bat mitzvah* ceremonies are properly planned—must be executed along with countless other synagogue activities. These all require the time and attention of the rabbi, Jewish educator, cantor, or executive director. Most are unable to design and implement new programs for conversion.

Creating a National Center for Jewish Inclusion

A National Center for Jewish Inclusion needs to be created. It should be the conduit through which a coalition of foundations and other funders promote conversion to Judaism. The National Center for Jewish Inclusion should be a clearinghouse for information on successful conversion curricula that currently exist. It should also work with seminaries, universities, and Judaic study programs to create new curricula and programmatic designs for use in synagogues, Jewish community centers, family services, Hillels, and other institutions that can become involved in promoting conversion. It should serve as a coordinating institution to help develop partnerships and coalitions among existing institutions so that they can coordinate to promote conversion.

The National Center for Jewish Inclusion must specifically address the issue of training rabbis to be better ambassadors for Judaism. Three specific approaches are necessary:

1. A rabbinic curriculum should be developed on how best to facilitate conversion (what to say, what to do). Much greater understanding, knowledge, and sensitivity about the thoughts and feelings of potential converts is necessary. This curriculum has to stipulate required courses in all the seminaries before rabbis go into the field.

2. Workshops, seminars, and other continuing education opportunities should be developed for the thousands of rabbis who are already in the field. These educational opportunities should be available at the local level, and free of charge. No rabbi should be deterred, by barriers of inconvenience or cost, from participating in learning how to encourage conversion. How we welcome and teach rabbis should be a model for how we welcome and teach converts.

3. A special training program at the national level should identify, recruit, and train the most promising rabbis who can promote conversion. They should be selected according to criteria of personality and knowledge, to find those who can best represent and encourage Judaism. This rabbinic core comprises the emissaries who also train their lay counterparts to be advocates for Judaism. They must be able to teach courses on how to teach Judaism, how to promote Judaism with others. They should receive special stipends and be supported to attend a retreat each year to meet with colleagues. We assume that constant learning and reinforcement in this arena is necessary.

The National Center for Jewish Inclusion would work with the denominational movements and other Jewish organizations and agencies to implement a national agenda for conversion. It would see that conversion becomes part of the national, regional, and local conferences held by the Union of American Hebrew Congregations, the United Synagogue for Conservative Judaism, and the Jewish Community Centers Association, for example. In any five-year period, tens of thousands of individuals who are active in synagogues and other Jewish organizations attend conferences to learn about how to build Jewish life in general, and how to improve the quality of their own institution specifically. The National Center for Jewish Inclusion must have a corps of advocates who can speak knowledgeably, passionately, and persuasively about the whys, whats, and how-tos of promoting conversion. It takes time for individuals and institutions to absorb the idea of proactive conversion and learn how to do it most effectively.

The National Center must be nondenominational and not constrained by any particular branch of Judaism's internal politics. The center should begin by sponsoring the conferences, forums, workshops, and think tanks necessary to promote the intellectual framework and political legwork necessary to begin the conversion initiative. It should create a national hotline for use by anybody who is interested in learning more about Judaism; it should prepare the materials to send out to those interested in exploring Jewish life. Ultimately it should be the institution that helps create advertising promotions and campaigns through TV, the Internet, radio, and other media to help attract individuals to Jewish life.

A new center would promote research on conversion. For example, the community should undertake a national survey of Jewish attitudes toward conversion, and also examine how potential converts encounter the Jewish establishment.

The Internet is a key tool for promoting conversion, one that continues to grow in importance. The National Center for Jewish

Inclusion needs to have information available on the Internet about where one can go for conversion counseling, training, or the ritual of conversion itself. The same information should be available in Jewish newspapers, general newspapers, organizational bulletins, and on bulletin boards where Jews congregate and visit. The word needs to get out.

The National Center for Jewish Inclusion must have an endowment to support efforts by individual rabbis and synagogues to develop classes and advertisements, provide release time for rabbis to engage in conversion teaching, pay for books and courses, and so on. The conversion enterprise involves costs, and these costs have to be permanently endowed. Otherwise, the conversion agenda could get lost again among innumerable competing financial causes, purposes, and agendas in the Jewish community.

A second set of institutions should be created: conversion centers at the local level. They can be called educational centers, institutes for Judaism, or whatever nomenclature indicates that they are gateways to Judaism and open to everyone. These may be associated with a particular synagogue or consortium of synagogues. Conversion centers can also be freestanding, independent institutions devoted to helping individuals become Jews, with independent rabbinic and other professional staff. Within or without synagogues, conversion centers need full-time personnel. The agenda cannot be financed and run out of some individual's or institution's hip pocket.

Conversion centers can also perform conversion ceremonies. They must be able to work with a *Beit Din* and either obtain access to a *mikvah* or have their own. Large Jewish communities such as Los Angeles, New York, South Florida, Chicago, and Philadelphia require more than one conversion center. Some conversion centers have to be conceived in the way that Chabad operates, having emissaries in communities through the United States.

Rabbis Are Not the Only Ones

Rabbis are not the only people who should be involved in promoting Judaism. For some potential converts, connecting first with a social worker or psychologist may be more comfortable than with a rabbi. Because the move to Judaism often involves complicated personal and familial conflicts, compromises, confusion, and fear, individuals trained in counseling and therapy may be the best ones to help potential converts navigate these waters.

Judaism is also *doing*. Instructors and facilitators who can show someone how to cook for Hanukkah and Passover or how to light Shabbat candles can be vital links to Judaism.

Having volunteers who are willing to welcome potential converts is a critical element in the proactive conversion process. It is essential for volunteers to invite potential converts for Shabbat dinner or a Seder or to sit with them in synagogue. They can invite them to attend Jewish music performances or a screening of a Jewish film festival. Or invite them to come along on a visit to Israel. They need to engage them in every way they can in Jewish life. They must have the ability to speak passionately about being Jewish— telling their story to others. Rabbi Bradley Artson (1993) describes the phenomenon of creating advocates for Judaism:

> What breaks through popular indifference or hostility is coming into contact with average Jews who have been turned on and reoriented to Judaism and Jewish living. Because these passionate Jews are still functioning in "normal" professions and still living within "normal" neighborhoods, they aren't threatening and they remove the fear that one will become an anachronism, a fanatic, or an idiot. They possess a credibility that no rabbi, educator, or Jewish professional can ever attain. What works is not a special "message" (that's just another gimmick). It is the messengers that are special—we provide the

tools and the passion and the ability for congregants to
become exemplars of Judaism to their neighbors, friends, and
families [pp. 7–8].

Parents and grandparents need to be active advocates for Judaism
within the family. This requires knowledge of what Judaism is and
what it provides. Parents and grandparents are commanded to teach
their children diligently, but they ought to know something to teach.
It also requires parents and grandparents to live a meaningful Jewish life. There is little room for hypocrisy in insisting that children
be Jews while Judaism has little meaning within the family construct.
If one is encouraging the boyfriend or girlfriend, the fiancee, the
spouse, or the children of a mixed marriage to participate in Jewish
life, one must actually be living that same Jewish life to some extent.

Finding the Financial Resources

These changes require a huge financial jump-start. Federations,
foundations, and private philanthropists are either engines of great
communal change or brakes on innovation. Little investment has
taken place directly in programs to deal with intermarriage, and
even less to encourage conversion. Given the immense overall
expenditures of federations and foundations, investment for conversion programs would not even appear as a microblip on the Jewish communal radar screen.

Jewish foundations occupy a unique place on the Jewish organizational and institutional landscape. They have the capacity to
spark the most innovative change and exert the most influence,
both because mainstream Jewish organizations require their financial support and because foundation funding can create new organizations and institutions. At this juncture, very little in the way of
creative energy, ideas, or programming has flowed from the Jewish
foundation world to focus specifically on conversion. A number of
foundations have created initiatives to build Jewish identity pri-

marily through the traditional venues of Jewish education. These essentially mirror existing institutional priorities and systems.

We need a bold new initiative to create more Jews. A major foundation undoubtedly has to take the lead in forming this coalition of funders and provide the initial $50 to $100 million to begin the process of change. The effort to transform Jewish life through growth by conversion cannot be conceived of as a "grant" or funding for some existing institution to create marginally innovative programs. It must be a long-term initiative.

Opening the philanthropic doors requires a level of excitement and inspiration among donors that currently does not exist in the Jewish community. So much of the feeling about and reaction to intermarriage has been negative. It is hard for some philanthropists to believe that the battle is still worth fighting. Thinking about positive approaches and developing innovative institutions and programs for conversion could release all the revenue needed to transform Jewish life.

A Vision

There is no guarantee that such an initiative will succeed, but it offers the best and boldest alternative to our current obsession with intermarriage. Jews should not and cannot go backward. The shtetls of Eastern Europe, the neighborhoods of the Lower East Side, and the comfort of 1950s Jewish enclaves are gone. Building the new Jewish community of the future requires thinking about Judaism in ways that have not been possible for thousands of years. It is wonderful that the United States offers the opportunity to be safe and secure enough to think about growth and prosperity; the result is that we can reach out, rather than being a besieged and threatened people. Perhaps liberation will finally be realized when Jews feel strong enough to openly declare that Judaism is a faith tradition that welcomes others.

It is difficult to envision this change in the Jewish community, but this does not mean it cannot be achieved. Creation of the state of Israel was long held to be a moral, geopolitical, and geographical impossibility. Nations are not carved out of hostile territory, lost tribes do not go home, and great nations are not rebuilt two thousand years after they have been destroyed. Israel was impossible—and yet the world Jewish community longed for it, conceived it, and built it against incredible—indeed, almost insurmountable—odds.

Jews must again imagine the impossible, dreaming of a Jewish community of fifty million or a hundred million rather than the tiny world community of twelve to fourteen million that it has become. We must be bold and strong enough to think of ourselves as a mighty people, not small and threatened minorities struggling to maintain existence. We should use our economic, social, political, and cultural power to help ourselves grow. We must quit lamenting our successes.

To think of liberation, power, and flexibility as a curse and a failure is perverse. How tragic it would be if we turned our religious and political victories into a self-inflicted nightmare, with the pinnacle achievement of freedom marking the beginning of eventual disappearance. Do we really believe that Jews can survive only if the external environment isolates us or if we, in turn, can keep the gates to Judaism closed?

Vision and leadership are crucial. The kind of bold leadership that helped create the state of Israel or the infrastructure of human and social services in the American Jewish community must be turned to the endeavor to create more Jews. Developing a coalition of federations and foundations requires charismatic, diligent, and committed lay and professional leadership. This radical approach to conversion challenges every contemporary aspect of the Jewish community. For Jews to engage in an ideological and structural shift entails enormous risk. There is no guarantee that welcoming converts will work in the long run. Indeed, we may invest hundreds of millions and then billions of dollars in a communal debacle. As opposed to what? Circling the wagons? Crying about assimilation? Placing faith in Jewish education systems that create stasis in both numbers and creativity?

Proactive conversion can help revitalize the Jewish community. Rethinking the Jewish future without rethinking the communal approach to conversion is a communal death wish.

Actively promoting conversion is a process far beyond the current system of reluctant and grudging acceptance of those who can clear all the hurdles that a hostile institutional and organizational network puts forward for those who might consider being Jews. The models of success must become the norm, rather than the exception. If Judaism is going to continue to maintain itself as one of the world's great religions, it must have new adherents. We Jews cannot continue to protect our heritage as a birthright only. We must swell and reinvigorate our ranks. If Jewish peoplehood is strong, we will be able to open the gates. We will create an even more vital, living Judaism.

Resources

Information and Support

Conversion to Judaism Resource Center
74 Hauppauge Road, Room 53
Commack, NY 11725
(516) 462-5826
e-mail: inform@convert.org

Information and resources for people considering conversion to Judaism. Sponsor of the Conversion to Judaism home page. Provides free copies of brochures and pamphlets on many aspects of conversion. Offers for sale several books on conversion by Lawrence J. Epstein, prominent Jewish thinker and president of the center.

Choosing Judaism Resource Center
St. Louis, Missouri
(314) 432-0020, ext. 3754; (314) 432-5700, ext. 3435

A communitywide resource network for anyone touched by the issue of conversion. A joint effort of the Central Agency for Jewish Education, Jewish Family and Children's Service, Jewish Community Center, and Union of American Hebrew Congregations. Supported by the St. Louis Rabbinical Association.

Jewish Converts and Interfaith Network
Lena Romanoff
1112 Hagys Ford Road
Penn Valley, PA 19072
(610) 664-8112
http://www.intermarriages.com

A pluralistic network of support groups and resources for proselytes, converts, interfaith couples, and mixed families.

Education

Note: Contact a rabbi in your community for information about Introduction to Judaism courses and other study opportunities in your community. Additional resources include private tutors, non-congregational classes, and online studies.

Patti Moskovitz
269 Avocet Court
Foster City, CA 94404
(650) 349-1222

A Jewish educator who provides private tutoring for people interested in converting to Judaism.

Keruv Center at Valley Beth Sholom
15739 Ventura Boulevard
Encino, CA 91436
(818) 788-6000, ext. 655

A Conservative congregation in the Los Angeles area with a large, comprehensive education and outreach program for people interested in Judaism. See Chapter Eight for a full description.

Miller Introduction to Judaism Program
University of Judaism
15600 Mulholland Drive
Los Angeles, CA 90077
(310) 440-1273

A large, noncongregational, pluralistic approach to Judaism provided by the Conservative movement's University of Judaism. Offered every weeknight and on Sunday afternoons at various locations in the Los Angeles area. See Chapter Eight for a full description.

Center for Conversion to Judaism
Rabbi Stephen C. Lerner
752 Stelton Street
Teaneck, NJ 07666
(212) 877-8640 (New York)
(201) 837-7552 (New Jersey)

A noncongregational educational institution for people interested in converting to Judaism. Affiliated with the Conservative movement. Offers classes and private tutoring in Teaneck, Manhattan, Westchester County, and Chicago. See Chapter Eight for a full description.

Online Resources

Conversion to Judaism
http://www.convert.org

The central online resource for conversion to Judaism, providing information and advice for converts and potential converts. Contains links to over 130 rabbis of every denomination around the United States and Canada. Also provides information and links to

Jewish educators working with proselytes, Jewish educational cooperatives, and other educational resources outside of the denominational structure.

Jewish Commission on Intermarriage
http://www.uscj.org/intmar

Information on the Conservative movement's approach to intermarriage and conversion, including links to the United Synagogue home page and additional resources for interfaith couples and families.

UAHC William and Lottie Daniel Outreach Department
http://www.shamash.org/reform/uahc/outreach

Information on the Reform movement's outreach program, including resources for interfaith couples and families, people interested in conversion, and unaffiliated Jews. Links to information on Introduction to Judaism classes and additional resources about conversion, Judaism, and the Reform movement.

Jewish Outreach Institute
http://www.joi.org

Information and resources for interfaith couples and families, including links to outreach programs and conversion courses around the United States.

Friends of Ruth listserv

An online e-mail discussion group on topics of interest to Jews-by-choice and potential converts. Subscribe free by writing to <listproc@shamash.org> and include the message "Subscribe Friends-of-Ruth [your first name] [your last name]."

Havienu L'Shalom Discussion Forum
http://www.havienu.org/bbs/bbsrules.html

An online bulletin board discussing conversion to Judaism. For access, read the rules of the forum, then choose Conversion to Judaism from the pulldown menu, and click the Go to Forum button.

Conversion to Judaism Shared
http://www.geocities.com/Heartland/Hills/8943

A list of links to basic information on Judaism and conversion, including stories of converts, educational resources, and discussion groups.

Glossary

aliyah (pl., *aliyot*)   literally "ascent"; (1) being called up to say a blessing for the reading of the Torah; (2) moving to Israel

baal teshuva   a Jewish adult who returns to observance of the biblical commandments

bar mitzvah (male), *bat mitzvah* (female)   literally, "child of the commandment"; a thirteen-year-old boy or twelve-year-old girl called to read the Torah for the first time

Beit Din   three-person rabbinical court guided by *Halachic* principles

bris   a shortened version of the Hebrew phrase "Brit Milah," literally "covenant"; the ritual circumcision of a male child at eight days old, symbolizing the covenant between God and Abraham

daven   to pray

ger (pl., *gerim*)   a convert

gerut   conversion

goy (pl., *goyim*)   literally, "other"; a non-Jew

Halacha   compilation of scriptural laws constituting the Jewish legal system; hence *Halachic*, according to Jewish scriptural law

Hanukkah   literally "dedication"; festival, lasting eight days, to commemorate the rededication of the Temple in Jerusalem in 165 B.C.E.

havurah (pl., *havurot*)   a group or fellowship, generally for study of sacred literature, celebrating holidays, or other Jewish-oriented activities

Hillel   student-based organization, named after a great rabbinic scholar, that provides Jewish programming on college and university campuses

kashrut   the Jewish dietary laws; hence *kosher*, suitable for a Jew to eat

keruv   encouragement for mixed-married families to maintain their Jewish ties

kiddush   blessing over wine for meals, Shabbat, festivals, and holy days

mikvah   ritual bath used for purification purposes by brides before marriage, women after monthly menstruation, and converts during the conversion ceremony

minyan (pl., *minyanim*)   a quorum of ten Jews beyond bar mitzvah age, representing the Jewish people as a community, required for the recitation of all Jewish prayers

mitzvah (pl., *mitzvot*)   a religious commandment; there are 613 biblical commandments

Oneg Shabbat   a Sabbath evening gathering, often including a reception

Seder (pl., *Sederim*)   literally "order"; a ritual meal at Passover

Shabbat (also, *Shabbos*)   the Sabbath, from sundown Friday evening to sundown Saturday evening

Shabbaton   a retreat

Sh'ma   literally "hear" (first word of the statement); the principal statement of Jewish faith and belief, stating there is only one God

shtetl   literally, "little town"; a small, self-sustaining Jewish community in Eastern Europe in the nineteenth and early twentieth centuries

shul   literally, "school"; a synagogue

sukkah (pl., *sukkot*)   a temporary place of dwelling built during Sukkot, the harvest festival, to commemorate the wandering of the Jewish people during the time of the Exodus

Tanach   acronym representing the five books of Moses (Torah), prophets (Nevi'im), and writings (Ketuvim)

tefillin   phylacteries: leather straps holding boxes that contain the four biblical passages of the Sh'ma and wrapped around the arm and on the forehead in accordance with Deuteronomy 6:4–9 and 11:13–21

References

American Jewish Committee. *Conversion Among the Intermarried*. New York: American Jewish Committee, 1987.

American Jewish Committee. *1997 Annual Survey of American Jewish Opinion*. New York: American Jewish Committee, 1997.

Artson, B. S. "Outreach Is a By-Product, Not a Goal." *Sh'ma*, Oct. 1, 1993, pp. 7–8.

Baeck, L. "The Mission of Judaism." In L. J. Epstein (ed.), *Readings on Conversion to Judaism*. Northvale, N.J.: Aronson, 1995.

Bayme, S. *Outreach to the Unaffiliated: Communal Context and Policy Direction*. New York: American Jewish Committee, Institute of Human Relations, 1992.

Bayme, S. "Intermarriage and Communal Policy: Prevention, Conversion, and Outreach." In A. Miller, J. Marder, and S. Bayme (eds.), *Approaches to Intermarriage: Areas of Consensus*. New York: American Jewish Committee, 1993.

Beiser, V. "Intermarried with Children." *Jerusalem Report*, Sept. 5, 1996, pp. 26–30.

Beiser, V. "Wanted: New Jews." *Jerusalem Report*, Feb. 20, 1997, pp. 30–35.

Benson, L. R. "From Outrage to Outreach." *Baltimore Jewish Times Special Supplement*, 1992, pp. 68–75, 84.

Berkowitz, A. L., and Moskovitz, P. (eds). *Embracing the Covenant: Converts to Judaism Talk About How and Why.* Woodstock, Vt.: Jewish Lights, 1996.

Central Conference of American Rabbis Committee on Conversion. "Proposed Guidelines for Rabbis Working with Prospective Jews-by-Choice." Draft 4, June 29, 1998.

Commission on Reform Jewish Outreach. "What Is Reform Jewish Outreach?" New York: Union of American Hebrew Congregations, 1997.

Commission on Reform Jewish Outreach. "Enrollment Policies in Reform Religious Schools." New York: Union of American Hebrew Congregations, n.d. (a).

Commission on Reform Jewish Outreach. "The Outreach Fellows Program for Conversion Certification." Union of American Hebrew Congregations, n.d. (b).

Cornell, G. W. "Rabbi Leads Drive to Reclaim 'Marginal Jews.'" *St. Louis Post-Dispatch*, Oct. 19, 1991, p. 10A.

Council of Jewish Federations. *1990 National Jewish Population Study.* New York: Council of Jewish Federations, 1992.

Council of Jewish Federations, Planning and Resource Development Department. *Outreach: Building Connections with Unaffiliated and Inactive Jews. Part 2: A Cross-Section of Programs in Large and Intermediate Jewish Communities.* New York: Council of Jewish Federations, 1992.

Epstein, J. "Foreword." In A. Silverstein, *It All Begins with a Date: Jewish Concerns About Intermarriage.* Northvale, N.J.: Aronson, 1995.

Epstein, L. J. *Conversion to Judaism: A Guidebook.* Northvale, N.J.: Aronson, 1994.

Epstein, L. J. (ed.). *Readings on Conversion to Judaism.* Northvale, N.J.: Aronson, 1995.

Fishman, S. B., Rimor, M., Tobin, G. A., and Medding, P. *Intermarriage and American Jews Today: New Findings and Policy Implications.* Maurice and Marilyn Cohen Center for Modern Jewish Studies, 1990.

Gerecht, A. (ed.). Newsletter. *Jewish Proclaimer,* 1998, 98(3).

Goldberg, J. J. "U.S. Jewry Pins Their Future on Education." *Jerusalem Report,* Oct. 6, 1994, pp. 26–31.

Gootman, E. "Black Converts Present a Poser to Return Law: Immigration Denied." *Forward,* May 15, 1998, pp. 1, 4.

Gordis, D. *Does the World Need the Jews? Rethinking Chosenness and American Jewish Identity.* New York: Scribner, 1997.

Greenberg, M. "A Problematic Heritage: The Attitude Toward the Gentile in the Jewish Tradition—An Israel Perspective." *Conservative Judaism,* 1996, 48(2), 23–35.

Horowitz, C. "Declining Birth Rates. Rampant Intermarriage. The 'Seinfeld Effect.' Are American Jews Assimilating Themselves out of Existence?" *New York,* July 14, 1997, pp. 31–37.

"Intermarriage." *William Petschek National Jewish Family Center of the American Jewish Committee Newsletter,* 1986, 6(2), 1–4.

Isaacs, R. H. *Becoming Jewish: A Handbook for Conversion.* New York: Rabbinical Assembly, 1993.

Kessler, E. J. "L.A. Steps Ahead of Israel." *Forward,* Feb. 20, 1998, p. 1.

Leadership Council of Conservative Judaism. "Statement on Intermarriage." Adopted Mar. 7, 1995.

Lerner, S. C. "The Introduction to Judaism Program" [syllabus]. Teaneck, N.J.: Center for Conversion to Judaism, n.d.

Mayer, E. *Intermarriage and Rabbinic Officiation.* New York: American Jewish Committee, 1989.

Mayer, E. (ed.). *The Imperatives of Jewish Outreach.* New York: Jewish Outreach Institute and Center for Jewish Studies, Graduate School of City University of New York, 1991a.

Mayer, E. "Why Not Judaism? Conversion Could Be the Answer to the Interfaith Marriage Problem." *Moment*, 1991b, *16*(5), 28–33, 39–42.

Mayer, E., and Sheingold, C. (eds.). *Intermarriage and the Jewish Future: A National Study*. New York: American Jewish Committee, 1979.

McClain, E. J. [E. Jaffe-Gill]. *Embracing the Stranger: Intermarriage and the Future of the American Jewish Community*. New York: Basic Books, 1995.

McClain, E. J. [E. Jaffe-Gill]. "Conversion: Reminding Us What Being Jewish Is All About." *Moment*, 1996, *21*(8), 30–35.

Medding, P. Y., Tobin, G. A., Fishman, S. B., and Rimor, M. "Jewish Identity in Conversionary and Mixed Marriages." In D. Singer and R. R. Seldin (eds.), *American Jewish Year Book 1992, Vol. 92*. New York: American Jewish Committee and Jewish Publication Society, 1992.

Miller, A. "Outreach to Intermarrieds: Parameters and Outlines." In A. Miller, J. Marder, and S. Bayme (eds.), *Approaches to Intermarriage: Areas of Consensus*. New York: American Jewish Committee, 1993.

"Netanyahu Angers Reform Delegation in Comments on Religious Conversion." *The Jewish Advocate* (Boston), June 19, 1998, p. 9.

Nguyen, L. "A Convert's Diary." *Forward*, June 26, 1998, p. 21.

Prager, D. "Judaism Must Seek Converts." In L. J. Epstein (ed.), *Readings on Conversion to Judaism*. Northvale, N.J.: Aronson, 1995.

Raab, E. "Anti-Semitism in the 1980s." *Midstream*, Feb. 1983, pp. 11–18.

Reconstructionist Rabbinical Association. *Guidelines on Conversion*. Approved at the Annual Reconstructionist Convention, Philadelphia, Jan. 1979.

Romanoff, L., with Hostein, L. *Your People, My People: Finding Acceptance and Fulfillment as a Jew by Choice*. New York: Jewish Publication Society, 1990.

Rosenbloom, J. R. *Conversion to Judaism: From the Biblical Period to the Present*. Cincinnati, Ohio: Hebrew Union College Press, 1978.

Sarna, J. D. "The Secret of Jewish Continuity." *Commentary*, 1994, 98(4), 55–58.

Sarna, J. D. "Reform Jewish Leaders, Intermarriage, and Conversion." In L. J. Epstein (ed.), *Readings on Conversion to Judaism*. Northvale, N.J.: Aronson, 1995.

Schulweis, H. M. "Seek Converts!" *Moment*, 1997, 22(4), 42–45.

Silverstein, A. *It All Begins with a Date: Jewish Concerns About Intermarriage*. Northvale, N.J.: Aronson, 1995.

Tobin, G. A., and Simon, K. *Rabbis Talk About Intermarriage: Implications for Communal Change*. San Francisco: Institute for Jewish and Community Research, 1999.

Tugend, T. "Top Conservative Rabbi Urges Mission to Convert Christians." *Jewish Bulletin of Northern California*, Nov. 15, 1996, p. 25.

Wertheimer, J., Leibman, C. S., and Cohen, S. M. "How to Save American Jews." *Commentary*, 1996, 101(1), 47–51.

The Author

Gary A. Tobin is president of the Institute for Jewish and Community Research in San Francisco. He is also the director of the Leonard and Madlyn Abramson Program in Jewish Policy Research at the University of Judaism. He earned his Ph.D. in city and regional planning from the University of California at Berkeley in 1975. He was the director for eleven years of the Maurice and Marilyn Cohen Center for Modern Jewish Studies at Brandeis University in Waltham, Massachusetts. Before joining Brandeis, he spent eleven years on the faculty of Washington University in St. Louis.

Tobin has worked extensively on patterns of racial segregation in schools and housing. He is the editor of two volumes about the effects of the racial schism in America, *What Happened to the Urban Crisis?* and *Divided Neighborhoods*.

He has been a planning and research consultant with Jewish organizations and agencies throughout North America. Tobin is the author of numerous books, articles, and planning reports on a wide range of subjects about Jewish life. He has published extensively in the areas of antisemitism, synagogue affiliation, Jewish organizational planning, and philanthropy in the Jewish community. His books include *Jewish Perceptions of Antisemitism* (1988) and *Church and Synagogue Affiliation* (1995, with Amy L. Sales). He is the coauthor with Kathy Simon of *Rabbis Talk About Intermarriage: Implications for Communal Change* (1999). Tobin is currently working on a book entitled

Philanthropy in the Modern Jewish Community. He is involved in research concerning racial and ethnic diversity in the Jewish community and Jewish family foundations. He received the Koret Foundation Prize in 1997 for his research in the American Jewish community.

Tobin and his wife, Diane, reside in San Francisco. They have six children: Adam, Amy, Sarah, Aryeh, Mia, and Jonah.

Index